Walk Around

MW00632600

MiG-21 Fishbed

By Hans-Heiri Stapfer
Color by Don Greer and David Gebhardt
Illustrated by Darren Glenn

Part 1

Walk Around Number 37

squadron/signal publications

Introduction

The Mikoyan-Gurevich **MiG-21** – codenamed **Fishbed** by the North Atlantic Treaty Organization (NATO) – resulted from a *Voenno Vozdushnye Sili* (VVS; Soviet Air Force) specification issued in 1953. Only 40 **MiG-21F**s (*Forsazh*; Boosted) (**Fishbed B**) were built in late 1959 before the **MiG-21F-13** (**Fishbed C**) entered production the same year. This was the first MiG-21 variant built in large numbers and it entered service with the 32nd Guards Fighter Aviation Regiment at Kubinka, near Moscow.

The MiG-21F-13 was a pure daylight interceptor equipped with a nose-mounted SRD-5M *Kvant* (Quantum; NATO codename Scan Fix) rangefinding radar. A 12,654-pound thrust Tumansky R-11F-300 two-shaft afterburning turbojet engine powered this variant, which was armed with a 30MM Nudelman-Rikhter NR-30 cannon mounted on the starboard lower fuselage. Two wing pylons carried R-3S (NATO AA-2 Atoll) Air-to-Air Missiles (AAMs) and air-to-surface weapons, including 240MM S-24 rockets.

Gosudarstvennyi Aviatsionnyi Zavod (GAZ; State Aircraft Factory) 21 at Gorky (now Nizhny-Novgorod) completed 606 MiG-21F-13s for the VVS between 1960 and 1962. Production then shifted to GAZ 30 *'Znamya Truda'* (Banner of Labor) in Moscow, where MiG-21s were built for export customers between 1962 and 1965. The Czechoslovak firm Aero completed 194 MiG-21F-13s under license at Vodochody, near Prague, between 1962 and 1972. MiG-21F-13s exported outside the Warsaw Pact had different Identification Friend or Foe (IFF) equipment and were designated **MiG-21F-12s**.

Mikoyan-Gurevich extensively redesigned the MiG-21F-13 for the second-generation variants. The **MiG-21PF** (*Perekhvatchik Forsazh*; Interceptor Boosted) (**Fishbed D**) had an enlarged nose for an RP-21 *Sapfir* (Sapphire; NATO Spin Scan) intercept radar. The 30MM cannon was deleted and armament restricted to AAMs and air-to-surface stores on the two wing pylons. Late production MiG-21PFs had wider chord (width) vertical stabilizers and brake parachute containers. GAZ 21 built the MiG-21PF for the VVS between 1962 and 1964 and GAZ 30 completed this variant for foreign customers between 1964 and 1968. India's Hindustan Aeronautics Limited (HAL) built the **MiG-21FL** – a modified MiG-21PF – under license at Nasik from 1966 until 1973.

The **MiG-21PFM** (*Modifikatsirovanny*; Modified) (**Fishbed F**) was a direct improvement of the earlier MiG-21PF. This new variant featured a fixed windshield and hinged canopy that opened to the right, which replaced the forward opening single-piece canopy of previous variants. GAZ 21 in Gorky built VVS MiG-21PFMs between late 1964 and 1965, while GAZ 30 in Moscow assembled export MiG-21PFMs between 1966 and 1968.

The earlier MiG-21F-13 was the basis for the first two-seat trainer variant, the **MiG-21U** (*Uchyebnii*; Trainer) (**Mongol A**). The second cockpit fitted aft of the original cockpit displaced some fuel. GAZ 81 at Tblisi, Georgian Soviet Socialist Republic (now Georgia) built 180 MiG-21Us between 1962 and 1966.

The **MiG-21US** (**Mongol B**) had a similar airframe to the earlier MiG-21U, but featured a retractable rear canopy periscope for the instructor. Avionics were upgraded to the standard of second-generation MiG-21s. GAZ 31 completed 347 MiG-21US trainers between 1966 and 1970.

The last Fishbed training variant was the **MiG-21UM** (also called Mongol B). It had upgraded avionics and equipment for conversion training on the third-generation MiG-21 variants (**MiG-21R/SM/M/MF**). From 1971 to 1975, GAZ 31 at Tblisi built 1133 MiG-21UMs for the VVS and for export customers.

Acknowledgements

A number of fellow friends and organizations contributed to this Walk Around. I express my sincere thanks to a number of people that assisted me in writing this volume:

Detlef Billig
Robert Bock
Stephan Boshniakov
Amelia Cachay
Robert F. Dorr
Nigel A. Eastaway
Marcus Fülber
Kerstin Gutbrod
Zdenek Hurt
Paul A. Jackson
Wilfried Kopenhagen
Helmut Kluger

Lubomir Kudlicka
Luftwaffenmuseum der Bundeswehr
Hans-Joachim Mau (†)
Andrzej Morgala
Klaus Niska
George Petkov
G. F. Petrov
George Punka
Russian Aviation Research Trust (RART)
Roman Sekyrka

Sergej F. Sergejev
Peter Steinemann
Wolfgang Tamme
Technik Museum Speyer
Zdenek Titz
Pavel Türk
Simon Watson
Jürgen Willisch

All photos by author unless otherwise credited.

ISBN 0-89747-483-X

If you have any photographs of aircraft, armor, soldiers or ships of any nation, particularly wartime snapshots, why not share them with us and help make Squadron/Signal's books all the more interesting and complete in the future. Any photograph sent to us will be copied and the original returned. The donor will be fully credited for any photos used. Please send them to:

Squadron/Signal Publications, Inc.
1115 Crowley Drive
Carrollton, TX 75011-5010

Если у вас есть фотографии самолётов, вооружения, солдат или кораблей любой страны, особенно, снимки времён войны, поделитесь с нами и помогите сделать новые книги издательства Эскадрон/Сигнал еще интереснее. Мы переснимем ваши фотографии и вернём оригиналы. Имена приславших снимки будут сопровождать все опубликованные фотографии. Пожалуйста, присылайте фотографии по адресу:

Squadron/Signal Publications, Inc.
1115 Crowley Drive
Carrollton, TX 75011-5010

軍用機、装甲車両、兵士、軍艦などの写真を所持しておられる方はいらっしゃいませんか？どの国のものでも結構です。作戦中に撮影されたものが特に良いのです。Squadron/Signal社の出版する刊行物において、このような写真は内容を一層充実し、興味深くすることができます。当方にお送り頂いた写真は、複写の後お返しいたします。出版物中に写真を使用した場合は、必ず提供者のお名前を明記させて頂きます。お写真は下記にご送付ください。

Squadron/Signal Publications, Inc.
1115 Crowley Drive
Carrollton, TX 75011-5010

(Front Cover) A Vietnam People's Army Air Force MiG-21PFM (Red 5066) intercepts a US Air Force B-52 Stratofortress over Thanh Hoa, North Vietnam on 13 April 1972. This Fishbed F was assigned to the 927th 'Lam Son' Fighter Regiment at Noi Bai Air Base.

(Previous Page) Hindustan Aeronautics Ltd. (HAL) built this MiG-21FL (C778) for the *Bharatiya Vayu Sena* (Indian Air Force). This aircraft was similar to the MiG-21PF, but had the broad chord tailfin standard on the later MiG-21PFM. A PT-21UK drag chute container is located below the rudder base. A Red cover is placed over the nose cone and engine intake. (Simon Watson)

(Rear Cover) This Afghan Army Air Force MiG-21PFM (Red 353) awaits its next mission during the 1980s. R-3S (AA-3 Atoll) air-to-air missiles are mounted on the wing pylons. Both the Afghans and Soviets employed MiG-21PFMs during the 1979-88 conflict in Afghanistan.

MiG-21F-13 (Fishbed C)

The MiG-21F-13 was the first Fishbed variant built in substantial numbers. In contrast to the predecessor model MiG-21F (Fishbed B), the left 30MM NR-30 cannon was deleted. Most Fishbed Cs were equipped with the SRD-5M *Kvant* (Quantum) radar rangefinder, known to NATO as Scan Fix. MiG-21Fs/F-13s were the only Fishbed/Mongol variants with the PVD air data boom mounted on the lower nose. Czechoslovak-built MiG-21F-13s lacked the glazed panel behind the canopy that was introduced on all Soviet-manufactured Fishbed Cs.

MiG-21PF (Fishbed D)

The MiG-21PF was an all-weather interceptor with an RP-21 *Sapfir* (Sapphire; Spin Scan) radar. Both the air intake and the shock cone were enlarged compared to earlier MiG-21s and the PVD-5 air data boom was mounted atop the air intake. Both centerline speed brakes were enlarged and repositioned higher on the lower fuselage. The antenna for the R-802V Very High Frequency (VHF) multi-channel communication radio was placed aft on the dorsal spine. Most MiG-21PFs were equipped with the narrow chord fin of 4.45 M2 (47.9 square feet). The MiG-21PF received the KT-92 (*Koleso Tarmaznoye*; Braked Wheel) main wheel with a larger diameter than the MiG-21F-13's KT-27 main wheels.

MiG-21PFM (Fishbed F)

The MiG-21PFM was the first Fishbed variant equipped with a fixed windshield and a main canopy hinged to open to the right. The MiG-21F-13/PF's SK ejection seat was replaced by a KM-1 zero-zero ejection seat. All MiG-21PFMs were equipped with a 5.3 M2 (57.1 square feet) vertical tail and a PT-21UK brake parachute container was mounted on the rudder's base. The MiG-21PFM was the first Fishbed version equipped with both the KT-102 nose wheel and the SPRD-99 Rocket Assisted Take Off (RATO) system.

MiG-21U (Mongol A)

The MiG-21U was the two-seat trainer variant of the Fishbed. This variant had a fixed windshield, in contrast to the forward-opening windshield of the MiG-21F-13 from which the MiG-21U was derived. Additionally, the PVD air data boom was mounted on the upper nose. MiG-21 trainer versions never carried a radar, resulting in these aircraft having the same nose dimensions as the MiG-21F-13. The MiG-21U employed the SK ejection seat installed in the MiG-21F-13.

MiG-21UM (Mongol B)

The MiG-21UM was the training variant for the third generation Fishbed family. It was fitted with an AP-155 autopilot, with a DVA-3 angle of attack sensor mounted on the left nose. An antenna mast for the R-832 VHF radio was located on the rear dorsal spine. In contrast to the third generation MiG-21 fighters with four underwing pylons, the MiG-21UM continued to have only two wing pylons.

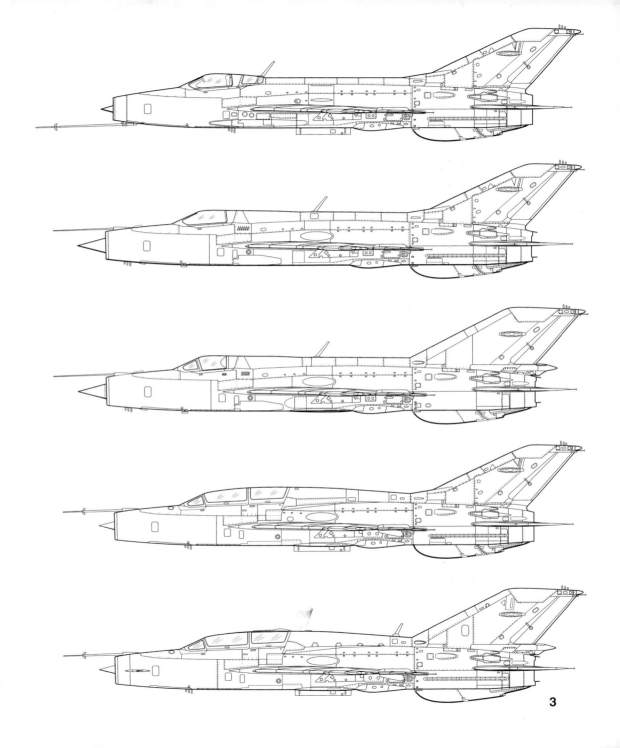

(Above) This camouflaged East German MiG-21F-13 (Red 639/Serial Number 74 19 22) flew with *Aufklärungsfliegerstaffel* (AFS; Reconnaissance Aviation Squadron) 31, which operated from Preschen Air Base, close to the Polish border. An AFA-39 camera was mounted in place of the starboard landing light. This particular Fishbed C was delivered in natural silver to the *Luftstreitkräfte der Nationalen Volksarmee* (LSK NVA; East German Air Force) on 1 August 1962. It previously served with *Jagdfliegergeschwader* (JG; Fighter Aviation Regiment) 8 *'Hermann Matern,'* JG 9 *'Heinrich Rau,'* and JG 3 *'Wladimir Komarow.'* While in service with the latter Fighter Aviation Regiment, Red 639 suffered an accident on 22 June 1967 but was repaired back into flying condition. The Fishbed C was camouflaged when it was reassigned to AFS 31. Upper surfaces were painted in Dark Green and Dark Brown, while a Pale Blue finish was applied to the undersurfaces. This MiG-21F-13 was removed from service on 15 October 1985 and scrapped on 23 October of the same year. AFS 31 was renamed *Taktische Aufklärungsfliegerstaffel* (TAFS; Tactical Reconnaissance Aviation Squadron) 47 on 1 November 1986. (Wilfried Kopenhagen)

(Left) A *Letectvo Ceskoslovenske Lidove Armady* (LCLA; Czechoslovak People's Army Air Force) MiG-21F-13 (Black 0418) is equipped with a centerline 490 L (129-gallon) fuel tank. This tank was safely used in all flight conditions up to a speed of Mach 1. No missile rails were mounted on the wing pylons. The solid metal part behind the canopy indicates that Aero built this particular Fishbed C at Vodochody, near Prague. Aero built 194 MiG-21F-13s for the LCLA in 11 blocks between February of 1962 and June of 1972. (Lubomir Kudlicka)

(Above) Ground crewmen prepare a *Fortele Aeriene ale Republicii Socialiste România* (FARSR; Romanian Air Force) MiG-21F-13 (Red 16) for a winter exercise. Two men pull away from the aircraft holding chocks pulled from in front of the main wheels. The PVD (*Priyamnikh Vozdushnyik Davlenii*; Air Data Boom) mounted under the nose was typical for the MiG-21F-13. This probe collected air ahead of the aircraft to feed into the flight instruments, including the speedometer. The TP-156M auxiliary air pressure tube was only mounted on the right side, just above the Red tactical number. (Author's Collection)

(Right) A Romanian pilot climbs into his MiG-21F-13 (Red 16) during a winter exercise. He wears a White GSh-4MS helmet for high altitude missions. A small White outline appears on the Red tactical number. A circular covering for the ARK-10 Automatic Direction Finder (ADF) is located between the PVD probe and the nose wheel well. This fibreglass item is painted Radome Green (FS24108). Two metal fore-and-aft coils behind this panel tuned to radio signals that were sent by ground stations. These signals aided in navigating the aircraft. The airflow spill door is mounted ahead of the tactical number. An identical door was also located on the opposite side. Hydraulic rams connected these doors to the engine inlet control system. These rams opened the relief doors to improve airflow in yawed (lateral) flight conditions and to avoid violent compressor stalling. (Author's Collection)

The pilot sits in the cockpit of an Aero-built MiG-21F-13 (Black 0207) assigned to the LCLA (Czechoslovak People's Army Air Force). Red bands on the natural metal PVD probe were unique to LCLA MiG-21F-13s. A Red covering protects the airflow suction relief door near the wing root. An external power cable led into the lower fuselage behind the KT-38 (*Koleso Tarmaznoye*; Braked Wheel) nose wheel. This cable fed power to the GSR-ST-1200-VT-21 Direct Current (DC) generator. The later MiG-21PF (Fishbed D) had its external power supply relocated to a position slightly under the wing leading edge. The blown acrylic canopy was raised to 50° using a pneumatic ram. This canopy was disconnected from the fuselage and protected the pilot in an ejection. A gun blast panel was mounted around the muzzle of the 30mm Nudelman-Rikhter NR-30 cannon, which was only mounted on the right side. The panel was made of steel, which better withstood the heat and pressure of the cannon firing than the aluminum alloy skin. (Zdenek Hurt)

A pilot prepares to launch in an LSK NVA (East German Air Force) MiG-21F-13s (Red 675/Serial Number 74 09 09). This Fishbed C was delivered to East Germany on 1 October 1963, but crashed during take off on 8 August 1968, killing the pilot. The tactical number was repeated on the 490 L centerline fuel tank. The second MiG-21F-13 in this row (Red 718/Serial Number 74 20 12) was removed from service during 1969 and is now displayed at the Military Technical Museum in Dresden, Germany. The TP-156M auxiliary air pressure tube above the tactical number was only located on the aircraft's right side. Most LSK NVA MiG-21F-13s had Black painted gun blast panels. The PVD nose probe's low position frequently resulted in damage by taxiing motor vehicles or inattentive ground crews. This resulted in the boom being repositioned on the upper nose on subsequent MiG-21 variants. (Hans-Joachim Mau)

The PVD air data boom was mounted under the nose on both the MiG-21F (Fishbed B) and MiG-21F-13 (Fishbed C). The temperature probe to the right of the PVD mounting fed data to the SRD-5M *Kvant* (Quantum; NATO designation Scan Fix) radar rangefinder mounted in the nose cone. This probe was repositioned to the left just aft of the nose wheel well on the later MiG-21PF/PFM.

Yaw vanes were fitted to the MiG-21F-13's PVD air data boom. These vanes were removed from the probe on the MiG-21PF (Fishbed D) and MiG-21PFM (Fishbed F), but reinstated on the third-generation MiG-21R/SM/M/MF (Fishbed J) variants. A retired *Bulgarski Voyenno Vozdushni Sili* (BVVS; Bulgarian Air Force) MiG-19P (506) is parked in the background.

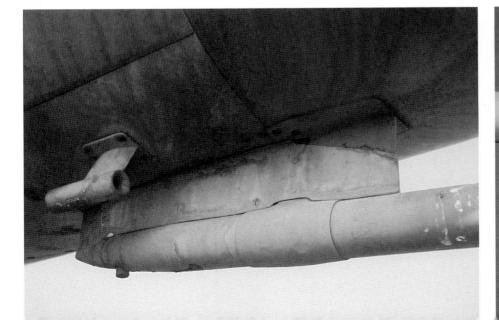

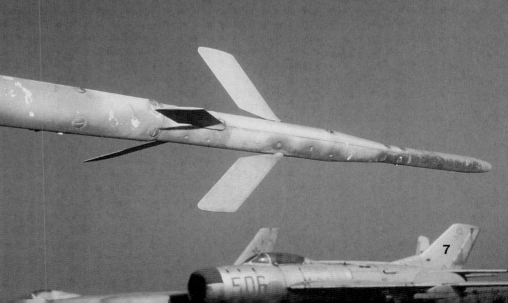

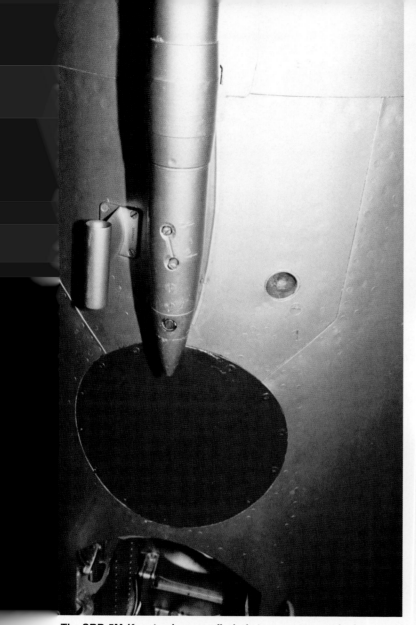

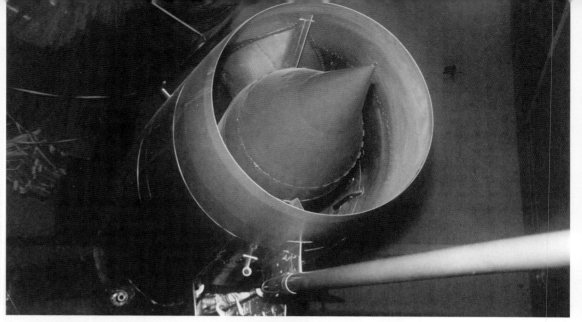

A cone housing the SRD-5M *Kvant* is installed within the MiG-21F-13's air intake. This cone slid in and out to decrease or increase the amount of air entering this intake, which fed the engine. A hydraulic actuator controlled by the air data system automatically operated the cone. Small tabs are mounted around the cone's aft section.

A streamlined fairing on the lower and upper air intake surfaces supported the intake cone assembly. Thin metal reinforcing arms fasten this assembly to the intake sides. This MiG-21F (Fishbed B) is displayed at the Technical Museum at Kiev, Ukraine. (Sergej F. Sergejev)

The SRD-5M *Kvant* radar rangefinder's temperature probe is mounted immediately right of the PVD probe. This boom is located on the lower nose of the MiG-21F-13. Immediately aft of the circular cover for the ARK-10 ADF. An unknown circular opening is fitted to the left of the PVD's base. This former East German MiG-21F-13 (Red

The right speed brake is fully deployed at 25° on this BVVS (Bulgarian Air Force) MiG-21F-13. The breech assembly of the 30MM Nudelman-Rikhter NR-30 cannon is located within the speed brake well. The speed brake's hydraulic actuator is mounted immediately below the weapon.

The MiG-21F-13's right speed brake had a circular gun gas vent just aft of the leading edge. This opening was not found on the left brake, which was otherwise identical in detail. The MiG-21F (Fishbed B) and MiG-21F-13 (Fishbed C) were the only variants to employ this pattern of speed brakes. All subsequent Fishbeds had

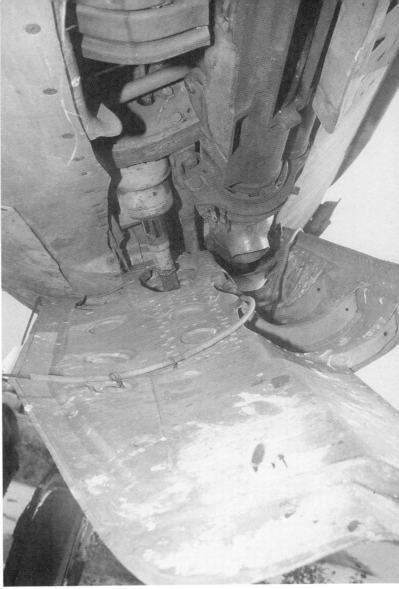

MiG-21F-13 pilots deployed their speed brakes to help slow the aircraft in flight, including during approach and landing. Each heavy metal forward speed brake had an area of 0.38 M2 (4.1 square feet). Speed brake inner surfaces and wells were usually left in natural metal or painted to match the aircraft's undersurface color – in this case, Pale Blue. This former BVVS MiG-21F-13 (White 501) is displayed at the Air and Space Museum at Krumovo Air Base near Plovdiv, Bulgaria.

9

The MiG-21F-13's 30mm NR-30 cannon was semi-recessed into the right lower fuselage. A large gun blast panel was mounted on the fuselage around the muzzle. Heated gases were vented from the gun through slots in the gun fairing. The earlier MiG-21F had a second 30mm weapon mounted on the lower left fuselage. This was removed on the MiG-21F-13 to allow room for air-to-air-missile avionics. An airflow relief door is located above the NR-30 fairing.

The extended speed brake exposes the NR-30's breech mechanism. Narrow slots in the adjacent fuselage panels allowed safe venting of hot gun gases that accumulated in this area. The ammunition feed chute runs from the centerline to the gun's breech. The MiG-21F-13's NR-30 was supplied with 30 rounds.

A gun gas relief opening is fitted to the MiG-21F-13's muzzle fairing. The 66.5 kg (146.6-pound) 30mm Nudelman-Rikhter NR-30 cannon was 2158mm (85 inches) long. It fired a 410 gram (14.5-ounce) round with a muzzle velocity of 780 m (2559 feet) per second. The NR-30's maximum cyclic rate of fire was 900 rounds per minute. The *Voenno Vozdushnye Sili* (VVS; Soviet Air Force) introduced the NR-30 into service in 1954.

Two 15STS-45A silver-zinc batteries were mounted immediately aft of the nose wheel well. An access hatch secured by 11 flush screws covered the battery component. A GSR-ST-1200-VT-21 DC generator charged the batteries during flight.

The MiG-21F-13's left speed brake slightly differed in detail from the right brake. A large fairing for missile electronics was mounted ahead of this brake. The fairing replaced the left 30mm NR-30 mounted in the earlier MiG-21F. The MiG-21F-13 lacked the left gun blast panel installed on the previous variant. This museum aircraft's asymmetrical brake deployment – the left brake retracted while the right brake is deployed – is not standard for the MiG-21.

The SRO-2 *Khrom*'s three-pole antenna was found on various Soviet military and civilian aircraft, including the Tupolev Tu-134 airliner. IFF employs coded radio signals from aircraft to determine their status as either friendly or hostile to other aircraft and ground or sea borne stations.

The left speed brake lacked the circular aperture located on the right brake. The three-pole antenna for the SRO-2 *Khrom* (Chrome; NATO codename Odd Rods) Identification Friend or Foe (IFF) system is mounted on the centerline. Only MiG-21F-13s built for the Soviet and Warsaw Pact air forces had the SRO-2 with this antenna. This IFF system was deleted on the MiG-21F-12 downgraded export variant.

MiG-21F-13s had the lower SRO-2 antenna mounted immediately in front of the speed brakes. This antenna was repositioned to the lower nose on subsequent MiG-21 variants. A circular hatch near the IFF antenna covered a socket for the auxiliary power supply, which fed the GSR-ST-1200-VT-21 DC generator. The second generation MiG-21PF/PFMs relocated this socket aft to a position just below the left wing leading edge

The MiG-21F-13's nose landing gear was equipped with a single KT-38 (*Koleso Tarmaznoye*; Braked Wheel). This wheel is mounted on a single vertical strut, which was supported on a freely castoring levered trailing fork. The gear strut assembly is painted a Light Gray, except for the chromed oleo (shock absorbing) strut near the trailing fork. The BVVS MiG-21F-13 displayed at Krumovo Air Base has the nose wheel placed on a plinth that reduced stress to the gear and tire.

The tire fitted to the KT-38 nose wheel measured 500ᴍᴍ (19.7 inches) in diameter by 180ᴍᴍ (7.1 inches) in width. Anti-skid drum brakes with two shoes are mounted on the KT-38. The pressurized feed line to the brakes ran from a pneumatic tank in the forward fuselage down the nose wheel strut. The MiG-21F, MiG-21F-13, and the MiG-21PF were the only Fishbed variants equipped with the KT-38 nose wheel.

(Above) The steerable KT-38 nose wheel was equipped with a UA-24/2M-5 anti-skid sensor beside the axle housing. This sensor was only mounted on the wheel's left side. The nose wheel castored a full 360° while the MiG-21F-13 taxied on the ground. The tire was embossed with its dimensions, 500mm by 180mm. The brake assembly of this MiG-21F-13 displayed at Dresden was left in natural metal, while the wheel rim is painted Blue Green (approximately FS25193), which was common on Soviet aircraft wheels.

(Right) This MiG-21F-13 had the landing gear strut and gear door inner surfaces in natural metal. This was normal when the aircraft was left in an overall natural metal finish. A Black electrical cable runs down from the gear well to the upper strut section. This cable supplied power to the PP-2 position light, which is not mounted on this displayed aircraft. Light from the PP-2 informed the ground crew watching at the runway's beginning that the MiG-21's landing gear was properly released.

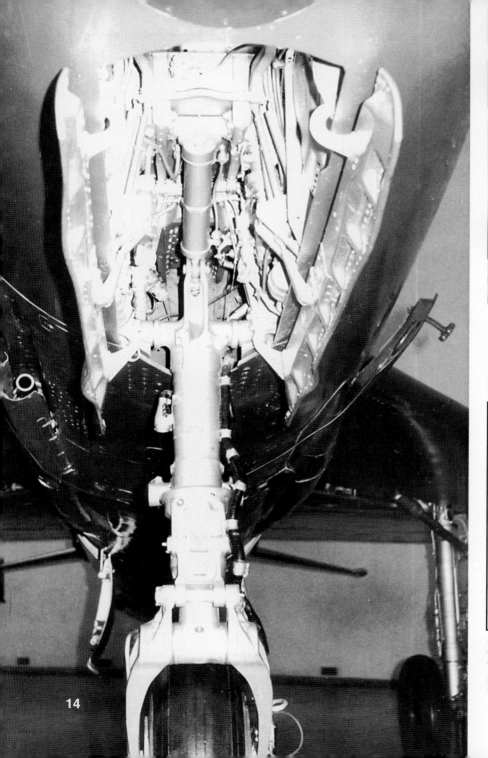

(Above) The MiG-21F-13's nose landing gear retracted forward into the narrow gear bay. Tubing for both the hydraulic and pneumatic systems ran along the lower gear well, immediately above the gear door opening. The primary hydraulic MiG-21 landing gear operation was backed up by a pressurized air emergency system. Nose gear doors were opened either mechanically or pneumatically in the event of a hydraulic failure. This pattern of nose gear door inner surfaces was only used on the MiG-21F and MiG-21F-13. Later MiG-21s employed different gear door inner surfaces.

First- and Second-Generation MiG-21s

VVS Designation	OKB Designation	First Flight	NATO Name
MiG-21F	Ye-6T, Type 72	1958	Fishbed B
MiG-21F-13	Ye-6, Type 74	1959	Fishbed C
MiG-21PF	Ye-7, Types 75 & 76	1960	Fishbed D
MiG-21PFM	Ye-7, Type 94	1963	Fishbed F
MiG-21U	Ye-6U, Type 66	1960	Mongol A
MiG-21US	Type 68	1967	Mongol B
MiG-21UM	Type 69	1971	Mongol B

VVS: *Voenno Vozdushnye Sili* (Soviet Air Force)
OKB: *Opytnoe Konstruktorskoe Byuro* (Experimental Design Bureau)

(Left) The nose landing gear strut is mounted in the MiG-21F-13's aft wheel well. Two doors covered this space when the gear is retracted. Three hinges secured each gear door to the well interior. These doors closed soon after the gear was retracted and opened just before gear extension. NP-34 M-1T pumps located in the fuselage generated hydraulic power for landing gear operation. Pressurized air was used to lower and lock the nose gear down in an emergency. (Wolfgang Tamme)

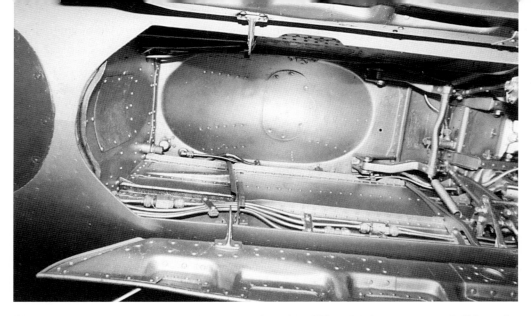

(Above) A cavity was located in the forward section of the MiG-21F-13's nose gear well. This cavity accommodated the KT-38 nose wheel and tire, which allowed for complete enclosure of the retracted gear inside this well. The doors' leading edges were angled to match the well's curvature. A portion of the ARK-10 ADF antenna housing is located immediately forward of the gear well.

First and Second-Generation MiG-21 Operators

Afghanistan	Finland	Pakistan*
Albania*	Georgia	Poland
Algeria	Hungary	Romania
Angola#	India	Slovakia#
Bangladesh*#	Indonesia	Somalia#
Bulgaria	Iran*	Soviet Union
Cambodia#	Iraq	Sri Lanka*
China*	Laos	Sudan#
Congo#	Libya#	Syria
Croatia#	Madagascar	Tanzania*
Cuba	Mali#	Vietnam (North before 1975)
Czechoslovakia/Czech	Mongolia	Yemen
Republic	Mozambique	Yugoslavia
East Germany	Myanmar*	Zambia#
Egypt	Nigeria#	Zimbabwe*
Ethiopia#	North Korea	

*Operated the unlicensed Chinese copy of the MiG-21, locally designated J-7 (F-7 for export) and its derivatives.
#Flew MiG-21U trainers alongside later MiG-21 fighter variants.

(Right) The PP-2 position light was mounted on the right side of this MiG-21F-13 nose gear strut. This light was a common feature on this MiG-21 variant. The lamp was only used to indicate proper undercarriage extension to the ground crew. Two high beam landing lights mounted in the wing undersurfaces provided the pilot with light during final approach and taxiing.

(Above) This MiG-21F-12 (Fishbed C) (MG-49/740409) was assigned to *Hävittäjälentolaivue* (HävLLv; Fighter Squadron) 31 of the *Ilmavoimat* (Finnish Air Force). Finland purchased 22 MiG-21F-12s from the Soviet Union, with the first ten arriving on 6 April 1963. This export standard aircraft lacked the SRO-2 *Khrom* IFF system used by MiG-21F-13s built for the Soviet Union and other Warsaw Pact nations. The *Ilmavoimat* assigned its Fishbed Cs to HävLLv 31 at Rissala. The Squadron's Black cat insignia is painted on the tailfin. The Finns lost four MiG-21F-12s in crashes during their service, which ended in the withdrawal of the last Fishbed C on 17 January 1986. (Klaus Niska)

(Left) The *Magyar Légierö* (ML; Hungarian Air Force) accepted the first MiG-21F-13 into service during 1962. Their first public display occurred during a flypast over the capital city of Budapest on 4 April 1962. *Gosudarstvennyi Aviatsionnyi Zavod* (GAZ; State Aircraft Factory) 30 *'Znamya Truda'* (Banner of Labor) at Moscow built all the ML's MiG-21F-13s. All MiG-21s built for export were assembled at GAZ 30. This particular Fishbed C (Red 301) carries a 490 L (129-gallon) fuel tank on the centerline fuselage. The external tank supplemented the internal fuel capacity of 2280 L (602 gallons) in early MiG-21F-13s and 2470 L (653 gallons) in later aircraft. An APU-13 missile rail mounted on the wing pylon accommodated one R-3S (AA-2 Atoll) air-to-air missile. The ML phased out most of their MiG-21F-13s from service during the early 1980s. (George Punka)

16

(Above) A UB-16-57 pod is mounted to the right wing pylon of an East German MiG-21F-13. This pod carried sixteen 57mm (2.2-inch) S-5 spin-stabilized rockets. Each S-5 was between 830mm (32.7 inches) to 1079mm (42.5 inches) long and weighed from 3.6 kg (7.9 pounds) to 5 kg (11 pounds), depending upon the subvariant. It had a 3.8 gram (0.1-ounce) hollow-charge warhead in the nose. The S-5's muzzle velocity varied from 450 m (1476 feet) to 725 m (2379 feet) per second.

(Above Right) Each UB-16-57 is attached to the wing pylon in six places, including anti-sway braces at the front and rear. The MiG-21F-13's tactical number (884) was painted on both the pylon and the rocket pod. The UB-16-57's aft section was removable for reloading.

(Right) Red warning stencilling in Russian (Cyrillic alphabet) is painted on the UB-16-57's rear section. Holes punched through this section allowed rocket exhaust to safely vent from the pod when the 57mm S-5 rockets were fired. A variety of Soviet-built aircraft – both fixed wing and helicopter – employed the UB-16-57, which was also widely used in the Warsaw Pact air forces. The signing of the Warsaw Treaty on 14 May 1955 formed this alliance. Warsaw Pact states included the Soviet Union, Albania (withdrew due to an ideological dispute in 1968), Bulgaria, Czechoslovakia, East Germany, Hungary, Poland, and Romania. This pact was dissolved at a meeting in Prague, Czechoslovakia on 1 July 1991. Bulgaria, the Czech Republic, Slovakia, Hungary, Poland, and Romania are now members of NATO.

17

The throttle is mounted on the MiG-21F-13's left console, just left and forward of the SK ejection seat. The light colored throttle handle had a white button for the R-802V Very High Frequency (VHF) multi-channel communications radio. Below the radio button is the speed brake actuation switch. Early MiG-21 cockpits were primarily painted Console Gray (FS26176). (*Luftwaffen Museum der Bundeswehr*)

Metal toggle switches for various electrical items are mounted along the right cockpit wall. The Black panel atop the console's center section houses controls for the ARK-10 Automatic Direction finder (ADF) system. The control stick has a textured Black plastic grip, which has weapons system control buttons at the top. (4+ Publications via Michal Ovcacik)

The MiG-21F-13's main acrylic canopy was hinged at the front to open forward. A 62мм thick bulletproof windshield is mounted immediately aft of the canopy hinge. An ASP-5ND gun sight is located right behind the windshield, with the AKS-5 gun camera mounted to the sight's right. Both the instrument panel and the control stick are painted Black, while a White vertical line is painted on the panel. The MiG-21F-13 instrument panel lacked the radar display found on the subsequent MiG-21PF. (4+ Publications via Michal Ovcacik)

(Above) Yellow (approximately FS33538) fuel pipes run under the rear canopy glazing of a MiG-21F (Fishbed B). Fuel ran from tanks immediately aft of the cockpit toward the engine through these pipes. The antenna mast immediately aft of this glazing supported the R-802V VHF radio. Two streamlined fairings covered locks on the main canopy's aft section. These fairings were also found on early production MiG-21F-13s, but were deleted on later production aircraft. (Sergej F. Sergejev)

(Above Right) The MiG-21F's rear glazing faired into a narrow spine atop the fuselage. This spine covered fuel pipes and control cables for the tail surfaces. NATO assessed this as a combat vulnerability. They were prone to damage from shrapnel. The SK ejection seat rests just below the main canopy's rear section. Aero-built MiG-21F-13s replaced the rear glazing with a solid metal panel. (Sergej F. Sergejev)

(Right) An LSK NVA (East German Air Force) ground crewman refuels a MiG-21F-13 (Red 718/Serial Number 74 20 12) for another mission. The Tumansky R-11F-300 turbojet required either T-1, T-2, or TS-1 kerosene. Canvas was placed above the wing surfaces to prevent damage by the ground crew. A Red cover is placed over the engine intake to keep Foreign Object Damage (FOD) out of this intake, while a crew access ladder is placed beside the aircraft. This MiG-21F-13 carries a single UB-16-57 pod on the left wing pylon. Fishbed Cs seldom used this conical version of the UB-16. This MiG-21F-13 was retired from service during 1969 and is now displayed at the Military Technical Museum at Dresden, Germany. (Hans-Joachim Mau)

The right aileron is slightly deflected upward on this MiG-21F. The later MiG-21F-13 had an identical wing. The wing fence near the wing tip prevented spanwise airflow that interfered with transonic (Mach 0.8 to 1.2) flight. A flap actuator fairing was mounted beside the aileron. A BU-45 hydraulic booster actuated the ailerons to +/- 20° deflection. (Sergej F. Sergejev)

A T-shaped antenna for the RV-UM low-range radio altimeter was mounted on each MiG-21F-13 wing. This device worked at low altitudes up to 600 м (1669 feet). Radio altimeters (also called radar altimeters) measured altitude using radio waves bounced from the aircraft to the ground and back. The antenna's conical end pointed forward the front.

A faded Bulgarian national insignia is painted on the lower right wing of this BVVS (Bulgarian Air Force) MiG-21F-13. Each wing had a 0.935 м2 (10.1-square foot) slotted flap for low-speed control. The flaps were track mounted and hydraulically boosted by two BU-45-servo-control units. Maximum flap settings were 24.5° for take off and 44.5° for landing. Each wing had 20 maintenance access hatches with screwed covers.

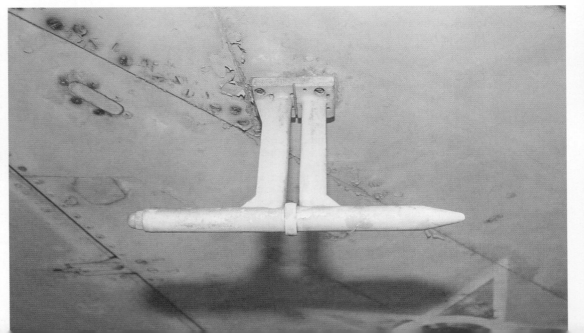

The MiG-21F-13's two wing pylons were each mounted outboard of the main landing gear. This pylon was not plumbed to carry external fuel tanks, unlike wing pylons introduced on third-generation MiG-21s. MiG-21F-13 wing pylons carried a variety of ordnance, including the R-3S (AA-2 Atoll) air-to-air missile and the UB-16-57 unguided rocket pod.

A static discharger was mounted on each MiG-21F-13 wing tip. It was used to remove static electricity that built up on the aircraft's surface during flight. A reinforcement panel was fitted to the lower wing tip.

A circular landing light was fitted into each lower wing surface just aft of the main wheel well. The pilot extended this front-hinged light while taxiing on the ground or while on final approach for landing. This lamp was retracted flush into the wing when not in use.

This track near the fuselage aided in moving the left wing flap. Additional tracks were mounted outboard of this flap and on the right wing. Pins mounted on the flap leading edge fit within the track for smooth travel to the take off and landing settings.

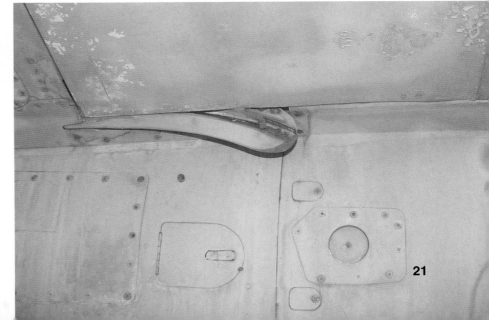

(Above) This MiG-21F-13's right main wheel door is opened for display. This door closed upward during gear retraction. MiG-21F/F-13 aircraft had this door configuration, which was changed to another rectangular shape on subsequent Fishbeds. The reinforcement rib arrangement in the main wheel well differed from the right and left gear wells on MiG-21Fs and MiG-21F-13s. The cavity inside the door accommodated the wheel and tire.

(Left) Each MiG-21F-13 main gear door was hinged fore and aft, with a hydraulic actuator on the well's front wall. The hydraulic piping layout in the right wheel well differed on the left side.

The main landing gear actuator is mounted in the leading edge of the MiG-21F-13's right wheel well. Secondary spars run spanwise and stringers run fore-to-aft on the well's ceiling. Three ball-shaped oxygen bottles are mounted in the outer aft well section.

The MiG-21F-13's left main wheel well had rectangular-shaped reinforcement ribs. These were in contrast to the bar-shaped ribs found in the right wheel well. A fuel hose runs into the forward well section, while hydraulic and pneumatic pipes and electrical cables run along the aft well surface. Wheel wells and door inner surfaces were painted Pale Blue (FS25550) on this Bulgarian MiG-21F-13.

The left main wheel well had a different hydraulic pipe arrangement than the right well. The compressed air bottle inboard and the three oxygen bottles outboard were in the same locations as on the opposite main landing gear well. Compressed air for the emergency landing gear release system was contained in the large bottle above the landing light. This natural metal MiG-21F-13 had its wheel wells and door interior surfaces kept in natural metal. The MiG-21F-13 had a track of 2692MM (106 inches) and a wheelbase of 4806MM (189 inches). (Wolfgang Tamme)

(Left) Each MiG-21F-13 main landing gear was fitted with a single KT-27 (*Koleso Tarmaznoye*; Braked Wheel) main wheel. The tire installed on this wheel was 660MM (26 inches) in diameter by 200MM (7.9 inches) in width. A pneumatic disc brake is mounted inside the KT-27 rim. This type of main wheel was only used by the MiG-21F and MiG-21F-13. A single door mounted outboard of the strut and hinged just above the tire enclosed the main wheel strut when retracted.

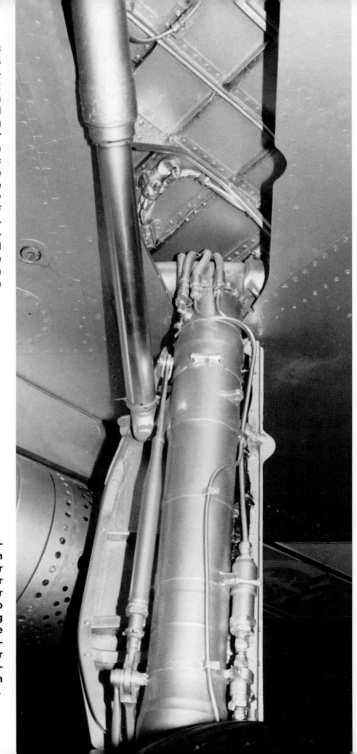

(Right) A hydraulic actuator ran from the main gear well to the upper section of the main gear strut. This actuator pulled the gear up into the main gear well. Wing spars and stringers are mounted in the well ceiling. Pressurized air released the main landing gear if the main hydraulic system failed.

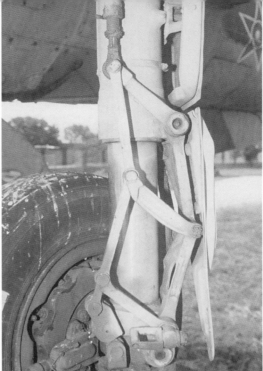

(Above) The 'Parallelogram' retracting mechanism was installed inboard of the KT-27 main wheel. This device was connected to the gear retraction system to synchronize wheel positioning during landing gear retraction and extension.

(Above Right) A UA-24 anti-skid system sensor is mounted on the main wheel's outer rim. An electro-pneumatic valve powered the anti-skid system, which prevented brake locking during ground operation. This Bulgarian MiG-21F-13's main gear is mounted on a plinth.

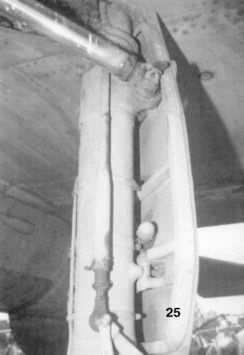

The KT-27 main wheel rotated 87° inwards during main landing gear retraction. This resulted in the wheel stowing near vertically into the fuselage wheel well. A complex mechanical linkage system called the 'Parallelogram' was installed at the bottom of the main gear leg. This device kept the wheels nearly vertical during retraction. Each main wheel was equipped with the UA-24 anti-skid braking system. Chocks are mounted forward and aft of the tire, while the gear is raised on a plinth for display purposes.

(Right) An HS-39 position light is mounted halfway down the inner main landing gear door. This position light let the ground crew know that the main gear was properly deployed.

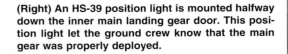

25

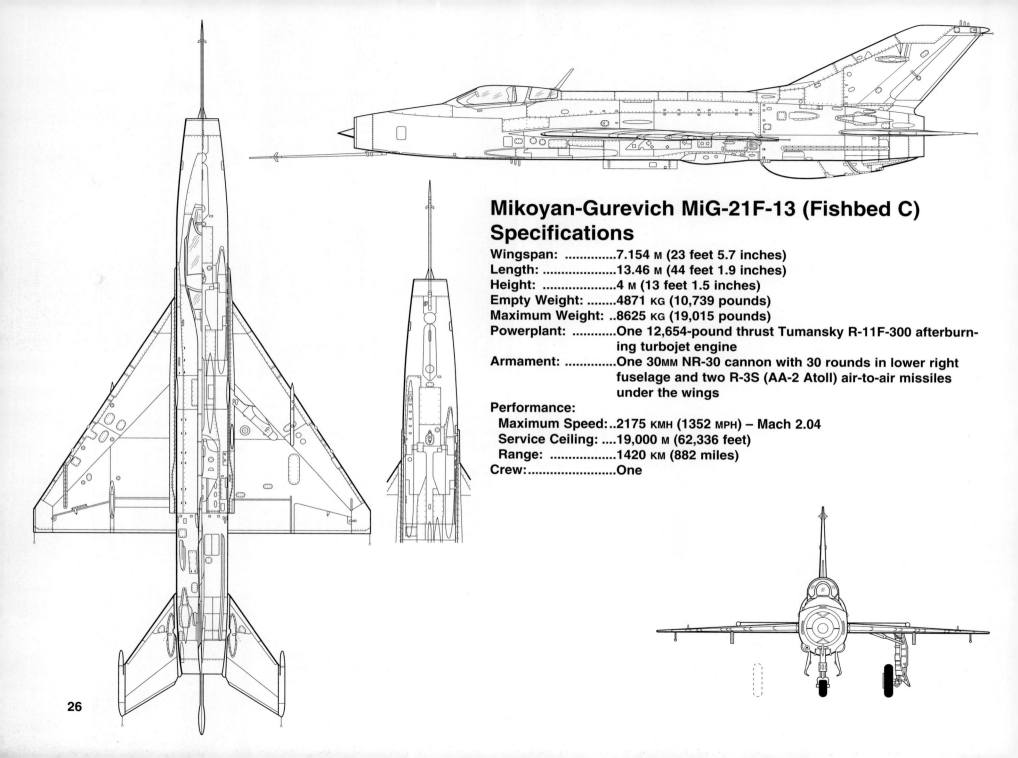

Mikoyan-Gurevich MiG-21F-13 (Fishbed C) Specifications

Wingspan: ....7.154 м (23 feet 5.7 inches)
Length: ....13.46 м (44 feet 1.9 inches)
Height: ....4 м (13 feet 1.5 inches)
Empty Weight: ....4871 кг (10,739 pounds)
Maximum Weight: ..8625 кг (19,015 pounds)
Powerplant: ....One 12,654-pound thrust Tumansky R-11F-300 afterburning turbojet engine
Armament: ....One 30мм NR-30 cannon with 30 rounds in lower right fuselage and two R-3S (AA-2 Atoll) air-to-air missiles under the wings
Performance:
  Maximum Speed:..2175 кмн (1352 мрн) – Mach 2.04
  Service Ceiling: ....19,000 м (62,336 feet)
  Range: ....1420 км (882 miles)
Crew:........................One

An Aero-built MiG-21F-13 (Black 1114) of the *Letectvo Ceskoslovenske Lidove Armady* (LCLA; Czechoslovak People's Army Air Force) rolls down the runway after landing. Its three speed brakes – two forward, one aft – are fully deployed and a 16 M^2 (172.2-square foot) circular drag chute streamed from the aircraft. This chute was housed in a PT-21 container mounted on the left rear fuselage. The LCLA reused this MiG-21F-13's tactical number (1114) on a later MiG-21M (Fishbed J). (Zdenek Hurt)

This two-part door on the lower left rear fuselage encloses the MiG-21F-13's PT-21 brake parachute container. A wire from the container ran aft to a hook located at the ventral fin's aft end. Ground crews always faced difficulties in properly stowing the parachute in the PT-21 container.

The drag chute anchor was located at the ventral fin's aft section on the MiG-21F-13 Fishbed C. This kept the chute cable secured to the aircraft when it was deployed. The pilot could cut this cable loose after landing to release the chute.

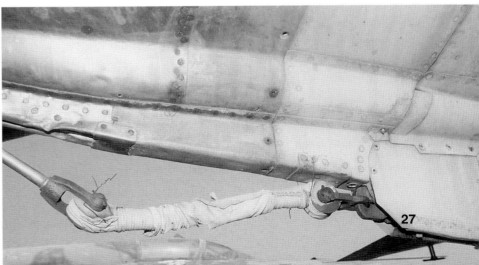

27

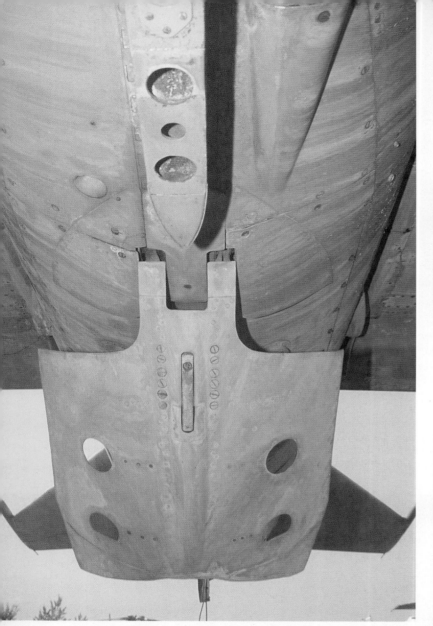

The MiG-21F-13's rear centerline speed brake had an area of 0.47 M^2 (5.1 square feet). It employed hydraulic operation, as with the two forward speed brakes. This aft brake is fully opened at a 40° angle from the fuselage. Four circular openings reduced buffeting when the brake was deployed.

One hydraulic actuator operated the MiG-21F-13's aft speed brake. A fuselage-mounted, engine-driven NP-34M-1T pump supplied hydraulic fluid for all three speed brakes.

This MiG-21F-13's rear centerline speed brake is deployed. This brake could not be employed when the 490 L centerline fuel tank was carried. This brake is mounted immediately aft of the centerline fuselage pylon. Mikoyan-Gurevich designers selected the three speed brakes (two forward and one aft) in order to maintain the aircraft's trim in flight.

This East German MiG-21F-13 has the 490 L fuel tank installed on its centerline pylon. This prevented deployment of the aft speed brake, although the two forward brakes were free to extend. An afterburner cooling inlet is placed on the lower right fuselage near the ventral fin's leading edge.

A hydraulic pipe fairing was mounted on the left rear fuselage of all MiG-21 variants, but not on the right side. The PT-21 brake parachute container doors are closed on the left rear fuselage of this Bulgarian MiG-21F-13. An RPCh telemetry antenna for transmitting key data on the aircraft's performance is located inside the ventral fin's forward section. This section is covered by Radome Green fiberglass.

The right side of the MiG-21F-13's ventral fin is a mirror image of its left side. A small fiberglass panel just above this fin houses the MRP-56P radio beacon receiver. This navigation device received radio signals from fixed ground stations, which determined the aircraft's position relative to that station. The MRP-56P was only located on the right rear fuselage.

A small inlet is mounted on both sides of the rear ventral fin. This vented cooling air into the Tumansky R-11F-300 two-shaft turbojet engine's nozzle actuator. The afterburner located just above the ventral fin burned fuel into heated exhaust gas, which increased thrust.

LSK NVA (East German Air Force) maintenance crews overhaul a MiG-21F-13 under a camouflage net. This is believed to have occurred during a Warsaw Pact exercise, when the LSK NVA practiced operating from forward airfields. Removal of the aft engine covering revealed the R-11F-300's variable convergent nozzle. The nozzle's opening varied based upon engine power and flight conditions. Two mechanics work on the hydraulic accumulator located in the lower rear fuselage. (Hans-Joachim Mau)

The R-11F-300's variable convergent nozzle was controlled by an electrically signalled hydraulic system. Three rams mounted in the 2, 6, and 10 o'clock positions drove the actuating ring. Three spray rings – including one immediately aft of the combustion section – sent fuel into the afterburner section. The R-11F-300's maximum thrust rating with afterburning was 12,654 pounds. Afterburning greatly increased fuel consumption; thus, MiG-21 pilots sparingly used this feature. A GSR-ST-1200-VT-21 DC generator started the engine. (Wolfgang Tamme)

The R-11F-300's nozzle was enclosed within a circular covering located at the aftmost fuselage section. This covering was made from titanium, which has greater heat resistant qualities than the aluminum alloy used for the vast majority of the MiG-21F-13's skin. An afterburning cooling air inlet runs from the ventral fin into the nozzle covering. This inlet was also found on the left side. The brake parachute anchor and cable are mounted at the ventral fin's aft end.

A Radome Green cone is mounted on the aft end of the MiG-21F-13's vertical tail cap. This cone houses the SOD-57M Air Traffic Control (ATC) transponder antenna, which broadcast the aircraft's signal to ATC radars. A static discharger is mounted immediately below this cone, with a position light underneath the discharger. The blister in front of the SOD-57M antenna was only mounted on the MiG-21F-13. Export model MiG-21F-12s lacked the *Sirena* (Siren) 2 radar warning receiver and the blister associated with this system.

A GIK-1 earth inductor compass fairing is mounted above the Hungarian national insignia on the MiG-21F-13's vertical stabilizer. A goniometer – an electrical transformer – in the GIK-1 generated current to read the earth's magnetic field, which determined the aircraft's direction. The SOD-57M ATC transponder fairing is located within the White vertical bar above the GIK-1 fairing. MiG-21F-12s exported outside of the Soviet Union and other Warsaw Pact nations lacked this item.

The GIK-1 fairing is also mounted on the right side of the MiG-21F-13's vertical stabilizer, including this camouflaged East German aircraft. A rudder lock fitted to the base of this rudder prevented this control surface from freely moving in the wind while the aircraft was parked. The MiG-21F-13's rudder travel range was 25° each to left and to right. Engine nozzle hydraulic piping was contained within the long, narrow fairing on the upper fuselage. The small inlet above this fairing ducted cool air into the nozzle actuator.

A MiG-21PF (Red 503) of the *Magyar Légierö* (Hungarian Air Force) sits on the ramp between missions. This Fishbed D carries a 490 L (129-gallon) fuel tank on the centerline fuselage. The tank was the same type used on the earlier MiG-21F-13 (Fishbed C). An APU-13 missile rail mounted on the right wing pylon accommodated an R-3S (NATO designation AA-2 Atoll) Air-to-Air Missile (AAM). The MiG-21PF was the first all-missile armed Fishbed variant, with the 30MM NR-30 cannon mounted on the earlier MiG-21F-13 deleted on the Fishbed D. (George Punka)

A *Fortele Aeriene ale Republicii Socialiste România* (FARSR; Romanian Air Force) MiG-21PF (Red 715/760715) performs an engine ground test. Two cables attached to the main landing gear secured the Fishbed D in place during this procedure. A 13,492-pound thrust Tumansky R-11F2-300 turbojet engine powered the MiG-21PF. An APU-13 missile rail for the R-3S AAM is mounted on the left wing pylon. The Romanian national insignia has a thin Blue outline, while a small White outline appears on the forward fuselage tactical number. (Author's Collection)

Late production MiG-21PFs received the broad chord fin that became standard on the succeeding MiG-21PFM (Fishbed F). This fin increased the vertical tail area from 3.8 M² (40.9 square feet) to 5.3 M² (57.1 square feet). The PT-21UK brake parachute container was located in a cylindrical fairing below the rudder base. Standard production MiG-21PFs housed this chute in the PT-21 compartment located on the left rear lower fuselage. The *Voenno Vozdushnye Sili* (VVS; Soviet Air Force) and the *Bharatiya Vayu Sena* (BVS; Indian Air Force) were the only operators of the MiG-21PF with the broad chord fin and PT-21UK brake chute housing. The BVS also operated the similar appearing MiG-21FL, which Hindustan Aeronautics Ltd. (HAL) built under license at Nasik, India. This VVS MiG-21PF (Red 22) taxis across a snow-covered ramp. A Radome Green fiberglass panel on the vertical stabilizer housed the R-802V Very High Frequency (VHF) multi-channel communications radio. This colored panel was not found on Fishbed Ds. (Author's Collection)

An LSK NVA (East German Air Force) MiG-21PF (Red 843/76 10 05) taxis at its base. The MiG-21PF was the first Fishbed variant with an all-weather capability. Its RP-21 *Sapfir* (Sapphire; NATO designation Spin Scan) radar required a major redesign of the aircraft's nose. Both the air intake and shock cone/radome were enlarged to accommodate the RP-21 set. A PVD-5 air data boom was mounted atop the intake, just ahead of the upper boundary air vent. The SRO-2M *Khrom-Nickel* (Chrome-Nickel; NATO designation Odd Rods) three-pole Identification Friend or Foe (IFF) antenna was repositioned to the lower nose section. A blister is mounted on the MiG-21PF's dorsal spine immediately aft of the canopy. This blister was not found on the earlier MiG-21F-13. The MiG-21PF did not carry any internal armament, although some aircraft had provision for a centerline GP-9 pod with one 23MM GSh-23 cannon and 200 rounds. Its pilot wears a ZSh-3 helmet and a KM-32 oxygen mask. The LSK NVA assigned this aircraft to *Jagdfliegergeschwader* (JG; Fighter Aviation Regiment) 8 *'Hermann Matern'* at Marxwalde on 1 May 1965. The East Germans planned to export this Fishbed D to the Islamic Republic of Iran, but the German Democratic Republic's dissolution on 3 October 1990 prior to the delivery date prevented this from happening. The Iranians had planned to assign this MiG-21PF to the *Pasdaran* (Islamic Revolutionary Guards Corps) Air Force. (Hans-Joachim Mau)

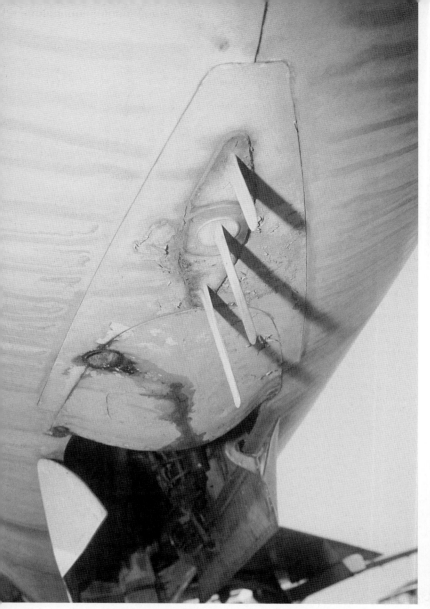

A Red intake cover is fitted to this *Polskie Wojsko Lotnicze* (PWL; Polish Air Force) MiG-21PF. The UVD-2M system ensured a steady control of the nose cone in all flight conditions. This cone extended 12.13 CM (4.8 inches) ahead of the air intake while the aircraft was on the ground. It was reduced to 2 CM (0.8 inch) ahead of the intake in flight. The Vozdukh LAS-1 *Lazur* (Azure) 1 Ground Control Intercept (GCI) system in the upper nose was introduced on the MiG-21PF. (Andrzej Morgala)

The MiG-21PF's enlarged nose resulted in redesigned nose landing gear doors. This variant lacked the small gear door blister found on the earlier MiG-21F-13. The MiG-21PF employed the same nose gear with the KT-38 wheel as the MiG-21F-13.

Both the MiG-21PF (Fishbed D) and MiG-21PFM (Fishbed F) used the SRO-2M *Khrom-Nikel* three-pole IFF antenna. This was mounted on a fairing just in front of the nose wheel well. The MiG-21PF was the first MiG-21 variant equipped with the modified SRO-2M IFF system. Earlier MiG-21F/F-13s were equipped with the SRO-2 *Khrom* (Chrome) IFF. The MiG-21F-13 had this antenna mounted behind the nose wheel well.

Making room for the RP-21 *Sapfir* radar resulted in a redesigned forward fuselage on the MiG-21PF. This included the nose landing gear well, which differed in details from the nose well on the earlier MiG-21F-13. An inspection panel is partially opened on the well's front wall on this BVVS (Bulgarian Air Force) MiG-21PF. Two hydraulic or pneumatic pipes and a dark electrical cable run across the front wall.

The MiG-21PF nose well has a deeper wheel cavity than the one on the MiG-21F-13. This adjustment was made due to the Fishbed D's larger nose and forward fuselage. Well support frames run down the left and right sides from the ceiling to the lower fuselage. Two pipes run into the upper right ceiling (upper left in this photograph). Additional piping runs across the opposite side.

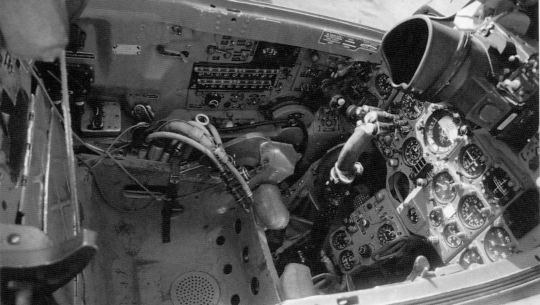

The Black throttle lever is mounted atop the MiG-21PF's left instrument console. Flap controls and the speed brake actuating lever are located near the throttle quadrant. Instruments above the throttle were connected with the Vozdukh LAS-1 *Lazur* 1 GCI system. (4+ Publications via Michal Ovcacik)

Controls for the RP-21 *Sapfir* radar and the ARK-10 Automatic Direction Finder (ADF) are mounted on the right cockpit wall. Radio and oxygen controls are located atop the console. Ground crews placed a clear panel on the aft wall section, which covered switches they only used during maintenance. (4+ Publications via Michal Ovcacik)

A scope for the RP-21 *Sapfir* (Spin Scan) radar is mounted atop the MiG-21PF's instrument panel. The PKI-1 gun sight is mounted above the radar scope and immediately aft of the bulletproof glass windshield. Instrument arrangements were generally similar to those on the MiG-21F-13's instrument panel. This Czechoslovak MiG-21PF's cockpit is primarily finished in Pale Peacock Blue (FS25299). Soviet researchers found this blue-green shade most soothing for its pilots. (4+ Publications via Michal Ovcacik)

The MiG-21PF employed the same 62MM thick bulletproof windshield as the earlier MiG-21F-13. It also retained the two smaller side windows attached to the windshield frame. The blown acrylic main canopy hinged forward immediately in front of this windshield. A pneumatic ram raised this canopy 50°. The RP-21 *Sapfir* radar scope with its rubber viewing hood is located below the windshield. (4+ Publications via Michal Ovcacik)

A Romanian pilot received congratulations from a colleague on completing a training mission in his MiG-21PF (Red 414/761414). The plate above the Type SK ejection seat was compressed downward when the canopy was closed, which armed the seat. Both pilots wear the ZSh-3 helmet. This SK seat's headrest is Black; however, most headrests were covered in Brown leather. (Author's Collection)

Both the MiG-21F-13 and the MiG-21PF used the Type SK ejection seat. This seat could only be used above 110 M (361 feet), since the parachute did not properly deploy below this altitude. This drawback led to development of the later KM-1 ejection seat. The pilot initiated ejection by pulling one of the Red handles that flanked the seat cushion. This activated a PK-3M-1 pyrotechnic cartridge, which started the TSM-2500-38 solid rocket motor. The SK ejection seat was equipped with an AD-3U time computer and the KAP-3 separation device, which separated the pilot from the seat 1.5 seconds after ejection. The maximum safe ejection speed was 1110 KMH (690 MPH). (Sergej F. Sergejev)

A Polish mechanic prepares a pilot for a night mission in a MiG-21PF. The PKI-1 gun sight is fitted above the RP-21 *Sapfir* radar scope atop the instrument panel. This Fishbed pilot wears a GSh-6M helmet for high altitude interception missions. The canopy disconnected from the fuselage in the event of an ejection. This canopy was ejected with the SK seat and acted as a blast shield for the pilot. (Andrzej Morgala)

A Polish pilot prepares for a mission in his MiG-21PF. The SK ejection seat was retained from the earlier MiG-21F-13. This Fishbed D pilot wears a GSh-6M helmet and a VKK-6 high altitude flight suit. Oxygen from the KKO-5 oxygen system was piped into the helmet's left side, while a communication microphone was mounted on the right side. Pilots regarded the VKK-6 pressure suit as highly uncomfortable. (Andrzej Morgala)

The canopy installed in early MiG-21s was secured using locks mounted at the aft frame ends. This is the left locking mechanism on a VVS (Soviet Air Force) MiG-21PF. The right mechanism was identical. (Sergej F. Sergejev)

The throttle lever is fully aft in the off position on this VVS MiG-21PF. This lever moved forward to increase engine power. Instruments for the Vozdukh LAS-1 *Lazur* 1 ground control intercept system are located above the throttle quadrant. A plexiglass bar covers buttons on the left cockpit wall that the ground crew set prior to a mission. This bar prevented the pilot from pressing these buttons in flight. (Sergej F. Sergejev)

The landing gear actuating lever is mounted immediately left of the MiG-21PF's instrument panel. A wheel-shaped knob is mounted at the lever's end. The pilot raised this lever to retract the landing gear and lowered the lever to extend the gear. Navigation system instruments are mounted on the console and on the instrument panel's left side. (Sergej F. Sergejev)

The open canopy reveals this MiG-21PF's cockpit. The PKI-1 gun sight was mounted just above the RP-21 *Sapfir* radar scope. The control stick is turned to the right, which exposed the instruments and controls located on the lower panel. This VVS aircraft had a Console Gray (FS26176) cockpit with a Black instrument panel. This was the scheme used on MiG-21s and other Soviet aircraft before Pale Peacock Blue replaced it in the late 1960s. (Sergej F. Sergejev)

Removal of the MiG-21F-13's 30mm NR-30 cannon resulted in a major redesign of the MiG-21PF's mid-fuselage section. The forward speed brakes were repositioned higher on the fuselage sides and their shape was changed. NP-34-1T hydraulic pumps inside the fuselage operated these speed brakes.

This MiG-21PF's right main wheel door is lowered. The main wheel doors and bays were redesigned on the Fishbed D over the units found on the earlier MiG-21F-13 (Fishbed C). This was due to the larger main wheels and tires installed on the MiG-21PF.

Various pipes and wires run down the rear wall of the MiG-21PF's right main wheel well. The Bulgarians painted this fuel pipe in wide Black and Yellow bands. Normally, fuel pipes were painted yellow on Warsaw Pact fighters. MiG-21PF wheel wells were finished the same color as the aircraft's undersurface – Pale Blue (FS25550) in this aircraft's case.

(Above) Various pipes run across the ceiling of the MiG-21PF's right main wheel well. Soviet and Warsaw Pact MiG-21s had fuel pipes in Yellow, although this Bulgarian aircraft had Black and Yellow fuel piping. Oxygen tubing was painted Blue, while Black pipes carried pressurized air. Use of color-coded piping aided ground crews, many of whom were conscripts.

(Above Right) The MiG-21PF's left main wheel well had squared reinforcements along its wall. This was in contrast to the vertical reinforcement ribs in the right main wheel well. The wheel door's hydraulic actuator was mounted in the forward wall and pulled the door up after the gear was retracted. The later MiG-21PFM (Fishbed F) retained the MiG-21PF's main wheel well configuration.

(Right) The MiG-21PF was the first variant equipped with the new KT-92 (*Koleso Tarmaznoye*; Braked Wheel) main wheel. This wheel was fitted with larger tires measuring 800mm (31.5 inches) in diameter by 200mm (7.9 inches) in width. The increased tire diameter required an enlarged wheel fairing on the fuselage. The KT-27 main wheel of the MiG-21F-13 only had a diameter of 660mm (26 inches), although their width was also 200mm. The MiG-21PF's larger tires were installed to cope with the aircraft's increased gross weight of 8770 kg (19,334 pounds), compared to the MiG-21F-13's 8625 kg (19,015-pound) gross weight.

A wing fence was mounted on the upper wing inboard of the MiG-21PF's wingtip. This thin surface kept air from flowing spanwise in low-speed flight and increased the control surfaces' effectiveness. A static discharger is mounted on the wingtip rear to dissipate static electricity generated on the wing.

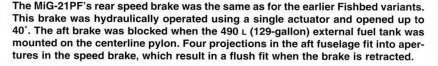

A T-shaped antenna for the RW-UM radio altimeter was mounted on each lower wing side. Unusually, the antenna on this Bulgarian MiG-21PF had conical ends on both sides of the horizontal antenna. The RW-UM usually had the conical area facing forward and the rounded end facing aft.

The MiG-21PF's rear speed brake was the same as for the earlier Fishbed variants. This brake was hydraulically operated using a single actuator and opened up to 40°. The aft brake was blocked when the 490 ʟ (129-gallon) external fuel tank was mounted on the centerline pylon. Four projections in the aft fuselage fit into apertures in the speed brake, which result in a flush fit when the brake is retracted.

An APU-7 missile rail is mounted on the left wing pylon of this Bulgarian MiG-21PF. The rail was used to for mounting the RS-2US (AA-1 Alkali) beam-riding Air-to-Air Missile (AAM) to the pylon. MiG-21PF carried either beam-riding RS-2US or the Infra-Red (IR) R-3S (AA-2 Atoll) AAMs, although the latter was more common in service.

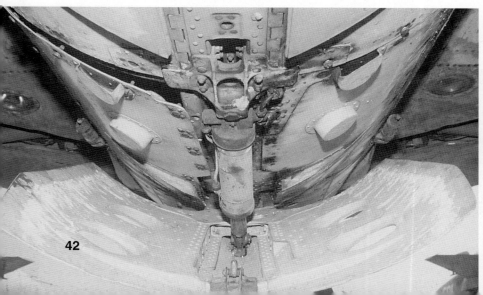

The MiG-21PF had the PT-21 brake parachute container located on the same lower left rear fuselage location as the MiG-21F-13. MiG-21PFs used both circular and cruciform (cross-shaped) brake chutes. This East German Fishbed D (Red 913/Serial Number 761114) ends its landing roll aided by an early circular brake chute. (Klaus Meissner)

Several PWL MiG-21PFs are lined up at a Polish air base. Anti-FOD (Foreign Object Damage) covers fitted over the R-11F2-300 engine nozzles were standard procedure when the aircraft were parked on the ramp. The narrow chord vertical tail was typical for most MiG-21PFs. A Radome Green SOD-57M Air Traffic Control (ATC) transponder is mounted above the Polish national insignia on the tail. (Andrzej Morgala)

This *Polskie Wojsko Lotnicze* (PWL; Polish Air Force) MiG-21PF (Red 2006/762006) comes to a halt using a later cruciform brake chute. This type of chute offered increased drag for slowing the aircraft, while keeping the canopy size down to fit the same PT-21 container. Brake parachute deployment upon landing stopped the MiG-21 after a 400 м (1312-foot) long landing roll. (Andrzej Morgala)

The RPCh telemetry antenna is mounted in the ventral fin's leading edge on this Bulgarian MiG-21PF. This section is in Radome Green fiberglass, along with the nearby panel covering the MRP-56P radio beacon receiver. This item was only mounted on the lower right fuselage. Above the MRP-56P panel is an afterburner cooling inlet, which was also only found on the aircraft's right side. This same inlet was mounted in front of the radio beacon receiver on the earlier MiG-21F-13.

Two PWL (Polish Air Force) MiG-21PFMs (Red 7903 and Red 7810) fly in close formation high above Poland. Neither Fishbed F carried a 490 L (129-gallon) centerline fuel tank. The lack of missiles on the wing pylons indicates that both aircraft were on a training mission. Most PWL MiG-21PFMs were assigned Red four-digit tactical numbers. The MiG-21PFM directly followed the MiG-21PF and featured a fixed windshield and sideways opening canopy. This replaced the front-hinged canopy installed on earlier Fishbeds. The wider chord vertical tail fitted to late production MiG-21PFs was standard on this variant. Additionally, a more powerful 13,613-pound thrust (afterburner rating) Tumansky R-11F2S-300 turbojet engine was installed. (Robert Bock)

A pilot enters the cockpit of a MiG-21PFM (Red 8011) of the *Fortele Aeriene ale Republicii Socialiste România* (FARSR; Romanian Air Force). The main canopy was hinged at the right for cockpit access. The MiG-21PFM was also the variant equipped with the improved KM-1 ejection seat developed by the MiG *Opytnoe Konstruktorskoe Byuro* (OKB; Experimental Design Bureau). The blister on the dorsal spine just aft of the cockpit was unique to both the MiG-21PF and MiG-21PFM. This aircraft and the adjoining Fishbed F were equipped with 490 L centerline fuel tanks. (Author's Collection)

Following pre-mission checks, FARSR mechanics hand off a MiG-21PFM to its pilot. Warsaw Pact MiG-21s lacked national insignias on the upper wing surfaces until the mid-1970s. Romanian national markings were painted on both the rear fuselage and the vertical stabilizer. A PT-21UK brake parachute container is mounted below the rudder base. The Radome Green fairing on the tail fin housed the SOD-57M transponder antenna. A White button-shaped *Sirena*-3M radar homing and warning system antenna is mounted just in front of the SOD-57M cone. (Author's Collection)

This former LSK NVA (East German Air Force) MiG-21PFM (Red 441/Serial Number 6709) was assigned to *Jagdfliegergeschwader* (JG; Fighter Aviation Regiment) 1 *'Fritz Schmenkel'* at Holzdorf. It arrived in the German Democratic Republic (East Germany) on 30 January 1968. This MiG-21PFM made the Regiment's final flight on 26 September 1990. The *Bundesluftwaffe* (Federal German Air Force) allocated the inventory number 22+02 to this Fishbed F. The Germans gave this aircraft a special paint scheme and Iron Cross national markings in April of 1991. This Fishbed F was nicknamed *'Weisser Hai'* (White Shark). The Germans planned to preseve this MiG-21PFM in a museum, but it was scrapped after 1789 total flight hours on 29 September 1992. (Werner Greppmeir)

Three Mongolian Air Force pilots stand before one (Red 002) of their 12 MiG-21PFMs. These late production Fishbed Fs were built with the TS-27AMSh rear mirror in the upper canopy. This allowed for deletion of the two small mirrors located on the canopy frame. Late production MiG-21PFMs had the RP-21MA's temperature probe relocated from slightly behind the left nose wheel door to slightly above this door. This location later became standard for the MiG-21SM/M/MF (Fishbed J) variants. Mongolia withdrew their MiG-21PFMs from service in 1993. (Wojciech Luczak)

This MiG-21PFM (Red 42) was assigned to the *Aviatsiya Voyenno Morskogo Flota* (AVMF; Soviet Naval Aviation). The Soviet naval ensign – White, with a Red star, Red hammer and sickle, and a Blue lower stripe – is painted aft of the tactical number. The MiG-21PFM was test flown at the Nitka Research and Training Complex at Saki (now in Ukraine) near the Black Sea. It was retrofitted with a TS-27AMSh rear view mirror in the canopy. The Radome Green fin tip dielectric panel housed the antenna for the R-802V VHF multi-channel communications radio. Camouflage colors for this MiG-21PFM are believed to be two greens and a brown over Pale Blue undersurfaces. (Andrej Zinchuk)

A PWL (Polish Air Force) MiG-21PFM is prepared for a mission. The hinged main canopy opened to the right and was secured by a canopy support strut attachment. The MiG-21PFM was the first variant equipped with two rear view mirrors in the canopy frame. These mirrors were also used on the later MiG-21SM/M aircraft. They were deleted on the MiG-21MF when the TS-27AMSh rear view mirror on top of the canopy became available. The MiG-21PFM was the first Fishbed variant equipped with the upgraded RP-21MA *Sapfir* (Sapphire; NATO designation Spin Scan) radar. (Andrzej Morgala)

The MiG-21PF and MiG-21PFM Fishbed F were the only Fishbed variants with small avionics bay cooling slots just under the left dorsal spine. These slots were not found on the earlier MiG-21F-13. The MiG-21PFM was the sole variant equipped with a venturi tube just in front of these slots. Airflow through this tube was used to drive vacuum instruments in the cockpit. The gun gas deflector plate below the airflow relief door was retrofitted to several MiG-21PFs and MiG-21PFMs.

The PVD-7 air data boom was secured to this platform on the MiG-21PFM's upper nose. This same platform was used for the MiG-21PF's PVD-5 boom.

The MiG-21PFM's PVD-7 air data boom was mounted atop the air intake. This boom was externally the same as the MiG-21PF's PVD-5 boom. Air data booms on these two variants lacked the yaw vanes employed on the MiG-21F-13's boom. The PVD-7 was mounted on the centerline, while later Fishbed variants had the boom offset to the right.

A 4 L (1.1-gallon) bottle of pure alcohol was stowed inside the upper nose boundary layer exit. Pressurized air was used to spray alcohol onto the windshield for de-icing purposes. A screwdriver was used to help open up this panel. Both the MiG-21PFM and the earlier MiG-21PF carried this de-icing equipment.

This former LSK NVA (East German Air Force) MiG-21PFM (Red 738) is now displayed at the *Technik Museum* (Technical Museum) at Speyer, Germany. The aircraft is painted in colorful Indian Air Force markings; however, India never flew the MiG-21PFM. The *Technik Museum* is the largest museum of its kind in Europe, displaying many Western and Eastern aircraft, rare trains, and automobiles from throughout the world. Part of a World War Two-era Dornier Do 24 flying boat is suspended above the MiG-21PFM.

The RP-21MA *Sapfir* radar's temperature probe was mounted just aft of the left nose landing gear door on both the MiG-21PF and most MiG-21PFMs. Late production MiG-21PFMs had this probe moved forward to a position slightly above the left gear door.

The MiG-21PFM (Fishbed F) was the first MiG-21 variant equipped with the KT-102 nose wheel. This had improved disc brakes for better stopping power on landing rollouts. A static discharge wire runs from the trailing fork to the ground. This allowed static electricity to escape from the aircraft's forward section, which eliminated electrical shock hazard to the aircraft and crew. The temperature probe for the RP-21MA *Sapfir* (NATO designation Spin Scan) radar is mounted just behind the nose wheel well.

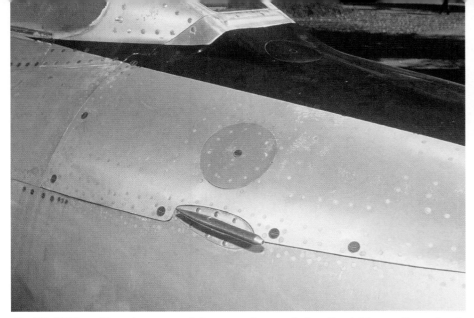

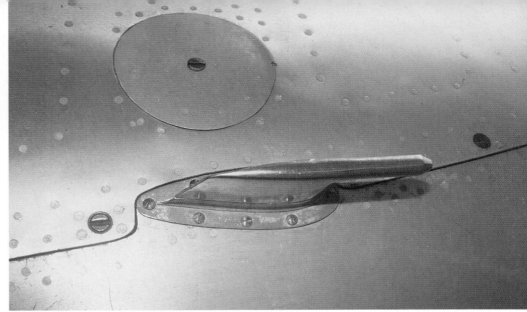

The TP-156M auxiliary air pressure tube was only mounted on the right nose. It was located just below a large avionics bay access panel. This provided access for the Vozdukh LAS-1 *Lazur* 4 GCI system, the R-802V VHF multi-channel communications radio, and the SRO-2M *Khrom-Nikel* (Chrome-Nickel; NATO designation Odd Rods) IFF system.

The canopy-opening handle is mounted just below the MiG-21PFM's left windshield. This handle was turned down to open the right-hinged canopy. No canopy-opening handle was mounted on the right side.

All first- and second-generation MiG-21 variants used the fuselage-mounted TP-156M auxiliary air pressure tube. This served as a pitot tube to collect airspeed data for cockpit instruments. The later MiG-21M/MF (Fishbed J) and MiG-21*bis* (Fishbed L/N) employed a pitot tube with a longer boom. The GA-8N22M gyroscope is mounted in a circular panel above the TP-156M.

A venturi tube is placed just below the left canopy and feeds the AD-6E cabin pressure regulation system. The MiG-21PFM was the sole Fishbed version fitted with the tube. No venturi tube was mounted on the right fuselage side.

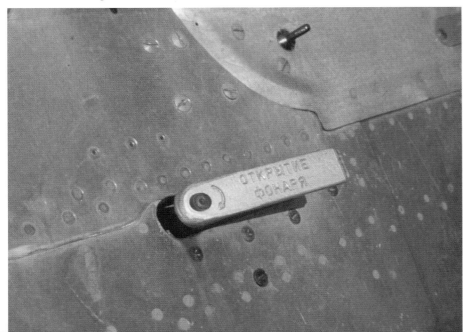

MiG-21PFM's instrument panel was virtually identical to that of the earlier MiG-21PF. The RP-21MA *Sapfir* radarscope with its Black rubber viewing hood is mounted on the panel's upper center section. Black air blast pipes for cockpit pressurization are located immediately below the windshield. Inflatable rubber canopy sealing on the cockpit sill is colored Canopy Seal Brown (FS20257). (Marcus Fülber)

RP-21MA radar control switches and knobs are mounted on the MiG-21PFM's right console. The Black panel above the console's front area housed ARK-10 radar compass instruments. A plexiglass panel covers switches on the cockpit side that are exclusively set by the ground crew before flight. (Marcus Fülber)

The throttle for the Tumansky R-11F2S-300 engine is mounted on the left cockpit console. A knob on this throttle operates the R-802V VHF multi-channel communications radio. Metal rings protect various switches on the wall, while two plexiglass bars cover those switches only set by the ground crew. These wall-mounted controls work with the Vozdukh LAS-1 *Lazur* 4 GCI system. The MK-16 pressure gauge is mounted on the aft cockpit wall. Covers were normally placed over the ORK-11 oxygen system tubes beside the seat when the MiG-21PFM was on the ground. (Marcus Fülber)

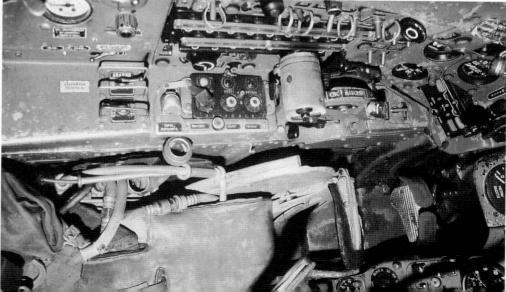

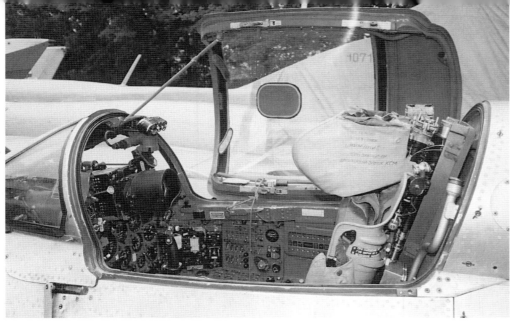

Two rear view mirrors are mounted in the MiG-21PFM's canopy frame. These mirrors were not fitted to earlier Fishbeds. This aircraft also has the center-mounted TS-27AMSh rear view mirror that was retrofitted to some MiG-21PFMs. This was the same mirror fitted to the MiG-21MF's canopy. Late MiG-21 variants did not have the two frame mirrors installed. The MiG-21PFM was the first variant equipped with the KM-1 ejection seat. (4+ Publications via Michal Ovcacik)

The NAZ-7 survival kit was packed in the KM-1 ejection seat's cushion. This kit included a knife, water disinfectant, waterproof matches, and three days' rations. An R-855UM radio beacon was also included in this kit.

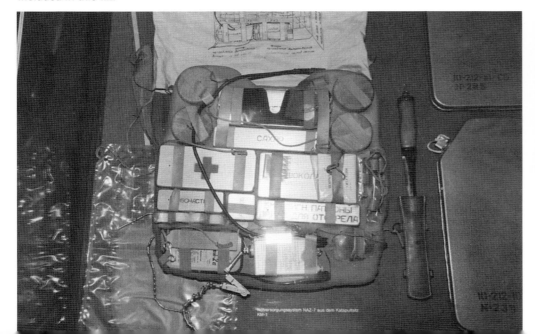

The RP-21MA *Sapfir* radarscope was mounted to the upper section of the MiG-21PFM's instrument panel. A flat Black circular visor was mounted over the scope. During daylight missions, the pilot bent his head into the visor, which shut out most exterior light and enabled him to clearly view the radar display. The ASP-PF-21 gun sight is mounted to the upper windshield frame immediately above the radarscope. (Marcus Fülber)

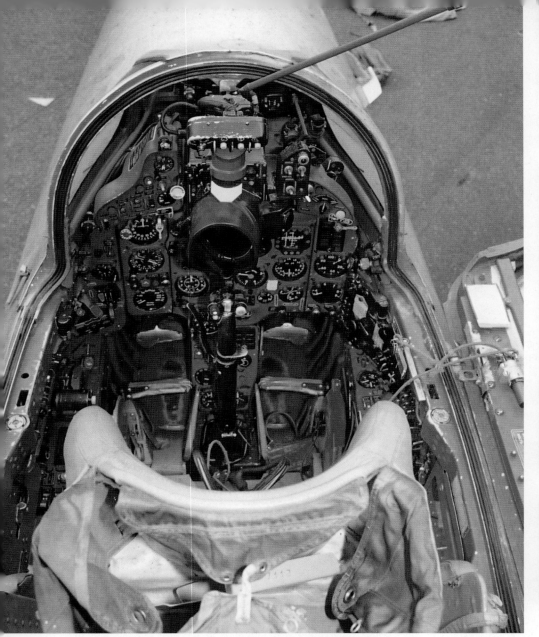

The canopy is opened on this Czechoslovak MiG-21PFM (Black 7113). A canopy stay arm is mounted at the windshield top. This arm kept the canopy opened to the right. The cockpit of this aircraft is primarily Pale Peacock Blue (FS25299). The radar scope's location immediately below the ASP-PF-21 gun sight was unique to the MiG-21PFM. (4+ Publications via Michal Ovcacik)

Primary flight instruments were mounted in the center section of the MiG-21PFM's instrument panel. Navigation displays were located to the left, while engine instruments were placed to the right. The master alarm panel on the upper right consisted of two rows of five White rectangular lights. These alerted the pilot to major problems on the aircraft. The radarscope at the panel's upper section was moved to the lower right panel area on the third-generation MiG-21SM/M/MF aircraft. Cockpit equipment frequently varied among production batches. (Marcus Fülber)

Automatic pilot separation devices are mounted in the KM-1 ejection seat's right side beside the cushion. These devices separated the pilot from his seat at a safe distance from the aircraft. The Silver manual separation arm was employed in the event of automatic device failure.

The NAZ-7 survival kit was packed in the seat cushion. The ORK-11 connector for the KKO-5 oxygen system is located on the cushion's left side. Two large Red ejection handles are mounted at the cushion's front end. The pilot initiated ejection by pulling up these handles. These handles were pushed forward to safe the seat, and pulled aft to arm it.

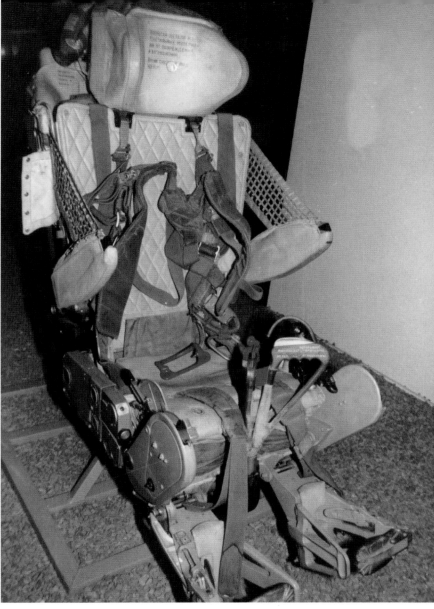

The MiG-21PFM was equipped with an early version of the KM-1 ejection seat. A 2 M² (21.5-square foot) stabilizing parachute is mounted inside the headrest. This combined with the PZ-1 rocket motor to pull the seat away from the aircraft. The pilot was automatically separated from his seat after a pre-set delay. The KM-1 allows safe ejections at speeds ranging from 130 to 1200 кмн (81 to 746 мрн). Safe ejections were possible up to an altitude of 25,000 м (82,021 feet).

53

(Above Left) A KT-92 (*Koleso Tarmaznoye*; Braked Wheel) main wheel is mounted on this East German MiG-21PFM (Red 841/Serial Number 5113). The UA-24/2M-5 anti-skid sensor is mounted on the outer rim in front of the axle. The diamond-shaped mechanism is part of the 'Parallelogram,' the mechanical linkage system that kept the main wheels nearly vertical when retracted. The KT-92 wheel was employed on the MiG-21PF and all subsequent variants. Tires lasted between ten and 30 landings, depending upon the severity of landings. (Helmut Kluger)

(Above) Polish ground crews removed the KT-92 main wheel and rim from a MiG-21PFM. This reveals the multiple disc brakes mounted inside the rim. Pneumatic and electro-pneumatic pipes run down the main landing gear strut. (Andrzej Morgala)

(Left) A White R-3S (AA-2 Atoll) infra-red homing Air-to-Air Missile (AAM) is mounted on an APU-13 missile rail. The Black serial number (R-A30103-310A-SB06) is painted on the missile's aft fuselage. The R-3S (also called the K-13T) was a Soviet copy of the American AIM-9 Sidewinder AAM. It was 2838MM (111.7 inches) long, with a diameter of 127MM (5 inches) and a weight of 73.5 KG (162 pounds), including a 9.5 KG (21-pound) warhead. (Helmut Kluger)

An R-3S is mounted on the right wing pylon of a Polish Air Force MiG-21PFM. The missile's serial number was repeated on the fuselage and the fin. Rollerons on the aft wings helped stabilize the missile's flight. The R-3S had a cruising speed of Mach 2.5 and a maximum range of 12 км (7.5 miles). (Andrzej Morgala)

A UB-16-57U rocket pod is mounted on an East German MiG-21PFM (Red 738/Serial Number 4301). This particular Fishbed is now exhibited at the *Technik Museum* (Technical Museum) at Speyer, Germany. This pod had a more conical front to the UB-16s carried by the MiG-21F-13. The UB-16-57U pod is loaded with 57мм unguided S-5M air-to-ground rockets. Red Cyrillic lettering on the pod's rear consisted of handling instructions. (Helmut Kluger)

The UB-16-57U pod is directly mounted to the BDZ-60-21D pylon. Each of the MiG-21PFM's two wing pylons could also carry one 500 кг (1102-pound) bomb. This pylon was not plumbed for carrying external fuel tanks. (Helmut Kluger)

This MiG-21PFM is equipped with a GP-9 gun pod on the centerline pylon. This pod was also carried on some MiG-21PFs. The GP-9 consisted of a 23мм GSh-23 twin-barrel cannon with 200 rounds of ammunition. This weapon has a muzzle velocity of 735 м (2411 feet) per second and a firing rate of 3600 rounds per minute. The GSh-23 is 1537мм (60.5 inches) long and weighs 50.5 кг (111.3 pounds). A circular external power socket is mounted just above the speed brake. (James Staley)

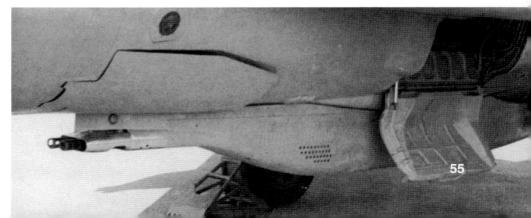

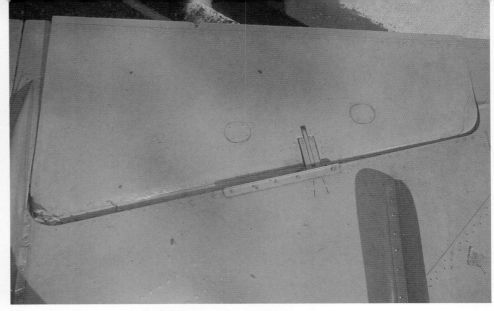

The MiG-21PFM's delta wing had a single fence only mounted on the upper surfaces. A red position light is mounted on the left wing's leading edge, while a green light is located on the right wing. A flap actuator fairing is mounted on the rear wing section where the aileron and the flap meet.

The BU-45A hydraulic actuator boosts the MiG-21PFM's ailerons to +/-20° deflection. This actuator is mounted on the aileron's leading edge, just inboard of the wing fence.

The aileron sway brace fairing protrudes from the MiG-21PFM's upper wing surface. A larger fairing covered the lower wing's aileron sway brace.

An airflow deflector bar is mounted on the aileron upper surfaces. This bar was not installed on the lower wing surfaces. All MiG-21 variants had this bar, which deflected airflow over the ailerons for more efficient operation of these control surfaces.

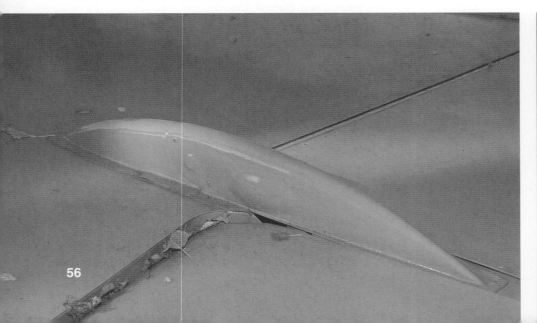

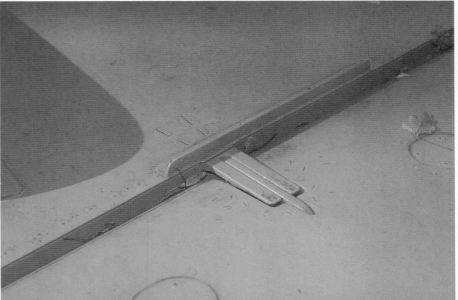

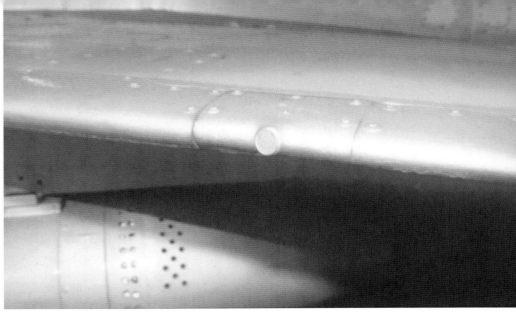

All first- and second-generation MiG-21s had identical wing leading edge position lights – red to left and green to right. A small dialectic panel outboard of the light covers the SOD-57M ATC transponder. This panel was normally Radome Green (FS24108), rather than the Silver panel on the *Technik Museum*'s MiG-21PFM.

The button-shaped SRO-2M *Khrom-Nikel* (NATO designation Odd Rods) Identification Friend or Foe (IFF) transmission antenna is mounted inboard of the wing position lights. This leading edge antenna and light configuration was carried over from the earlier MiG-21PF.

The retractable MPRF-1A landing light was mounted on both lower wing surface sides. This circular light is located just aft of the main landing gear bays. It extended forward when turned on by the pilot. The MPRF-1A illuminated the ground ahead of the pilot during final approach and landing. The MiG-21PFM exhibited at the *Technik Museum* had a replacement landing light manufactured by the American firm General Electric (GE). This was a replacement for the Soviet-built lamp installed at the factory. Three Blue oxygen tanks and a single Black pressurized air tank are located in the left main wheel well. The oxygen tanks supplied the pilot's oxygen system for high-altitude flying, while the pressurized air fed the emergency pneumatic landing gear retraction system.

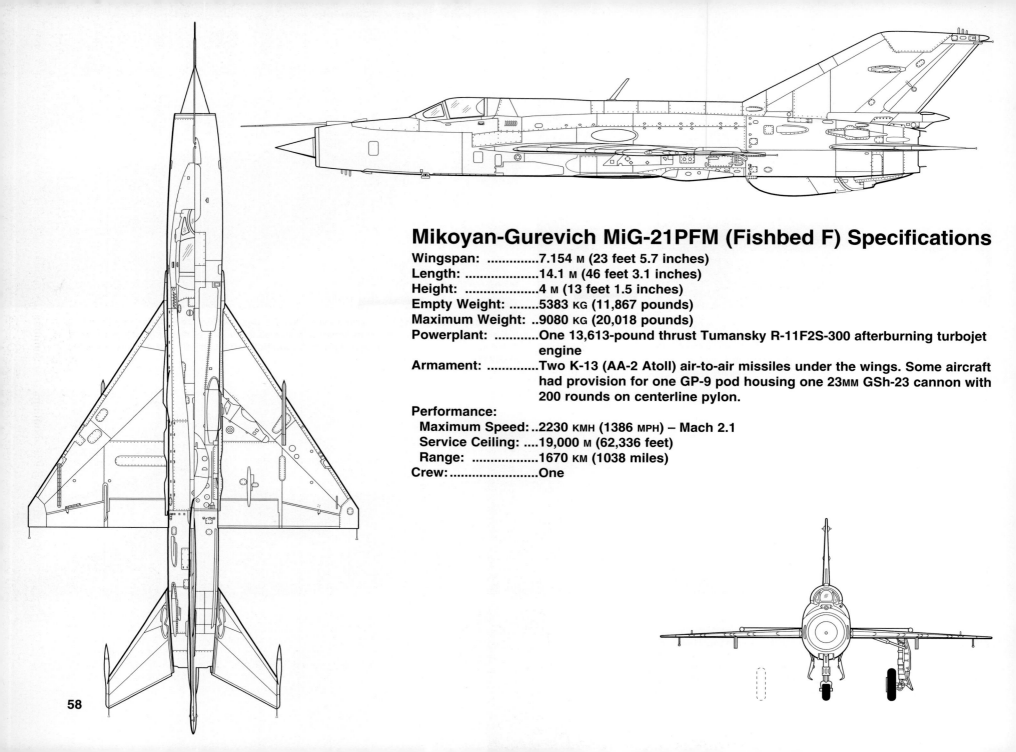

Mikoyan-Gurevich MiG-21PFM (Fishbed F) Specifications

Wingspan: ....7.154 м (23 feet 5.7 inches)
Length: ....14.1 м (46 feet 3.1 inches)
Height: ....4 м (13 feet 1.5 inches)
Empty Weight: ....5383 кг (11,867 pounds)
Maximum Weight: ..9080 кг (20,018 pounds)
Powerplant: ....One 13,613-pound thrust Tumansky R-11F2S-300 afterburning turbojet
engine
Armament: ....Two K-13 (AA-2 Atoll) air-to-air missiles under the wings. Some aircraft
had provision for one GP-9 pod housing one 23мм GSh-23 cannon with
200 rounds on centerline pylon.

Performance:
  Maximum Speed: ..2230 кмн (1386 мрн) – Mach 2.1
  Service Ceiling: ....19,000 м (62,336 feet)
  Range: ....1670 км (1038 miles)
Crew: ....One

Two SPRD-99 rockets assist in launching this LSK NVA (East German Air Force) MiG-21PFM (Red 730/Serial Number 4214) off a grass airfield. *Oberstleutnant* (Lieutenant Colonel) Ammer flew this aircraft on a Rocket Assisted Take Off (RATO), which sent the MiG-21PFM airborne in less than 200 M (656 feet). This Fishbed was assigned to *Jagdfliegergeschwader* (JG; Fighter Aviation Regiment) 8 *'Hermann Matern'* at Marxwalde. The RATO demonstration occurred during the 5th World Aerobatic Championship at Magdeburg, German Democratic Republic on 18 August 1968. This MiG-21PFM crashed on 30 May 1980, killing pilot Gerald Liebke. (Hans-Joachim Mau)

The front SPRD-99 rocket attachment point was located on fuselage frame 22. This was repeated on the right fuselage side.

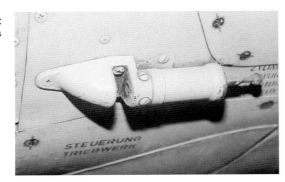

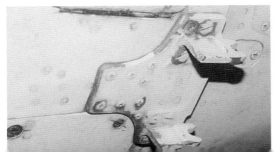

The rear SPRD-99 attachment point was mounted on the MiG-21PFM's frame 28. These left and right attachment points were identical on the second, third, and fourth generation MiG-21s.

An East German mechanic moves a Kartukov SPRD-99 RATO rocket on its transport and loading dolly. This solid propellant rocket had a thrust rating of 5510 pounds. The MiG-21PFM was the first MiG-21 variant equipped with RATO capability. After a successful take off, both SPRD-99s were jettisoned using a TKE-256PD electrical relay and a 695000-1 electro-pneumatic valve. This rocket could be used only once and was returned to its manufacturing plant in the Soviet Union for refurbishment. (Helmut Kluger)

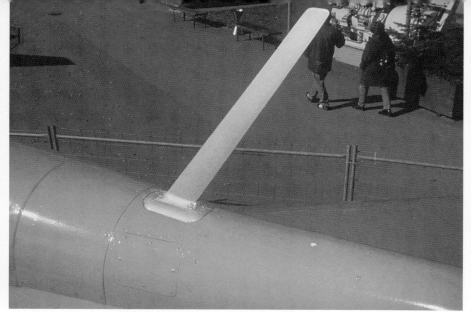

The MiG-21PFM's central refuelling port was identical to that on the earlier MiG-21PF. This circular refuelling port was located on the dorsal spine just aft of the canopy. Third-generation Fishbeds moved this port further aft along the spine. The centerline blister only found on MiG-21PFs and MiG-21PFMs served an unknown purpose.

Second-generation MiG-21s received external power through a circular port located on the left fuselage just under the wing leading edge. This was employed when the Fishbed was on the ground prior to engine start. Earlier MiG-21F-13s had this port located on the lower nose surface. Third-and four-generation Fishbeds had two such plugs installed in the same location.

Both the MiG-21PF and the MiG-21PFM had an antenna mast located on the dorsal spine. This mast supported the R-802V Very High Frequency (VHF) multi-channel communications radio. Third- and fourth-generation Fishbeds replaced this antenna mast with a fiberglass dielectric panel located on the vertical tail tip.

This MiG-21PFM was retrofitted with gun blast deflector plates on both fuselage sides. These plates helped prevent ingesting gun gases, dirt, or small stones during take off from unimproved airstrips. Some MiG-21PF/PFM aircraft had these plates added, since they were not standard on the production line. The MiG-21MF (Fishbed J) introduced these deflector plates as production standard.

The entire aft fuselage and tail section was removable from all MiG-21 variants. This feature allowed for quick access to the engine, which was the Tumansky R-11F2S-300 on the MiG-21PFM. This East German Fishbed F (Red 829) is jacked up for maintenance. The closed variable convergent nozzle is standard for a shut down R-11F2S-300. A Sukhoi Su-22M-4 (Fitter K) is parked behind this MiG-21PFM. (Marcus Fülber)

A panel with three slots had been located aft of the MiG-21PFM's main wheel well. This panel was only located on the right side of the rear fuselage on Fishbed Fs. The slots vented heated air from an avionics compartment.

Two attachment points for SPRD-99 RATO rockets are mounted on the rear lower section of the MiG-21PFM's fuselage. The rear speed brake is lowered due to a lack of hydraulic pressure. This brake was normally retracted when engine power activated hydraulic pressure.

Three hydraulic actuators operate the Tumansky R-11F2S-300's variable convergent nozzle. Two PWL mechanics check this nozzle during a periodic overhaul. The R-11F2S-300 had a second pilot selectable stage of afterburner, which reduced acceleration times to supersonic speeds. (Andrzej Morgala)

Mechanics removed the tail from a PWL MiG-21PFM during a general overhaul. The rear speed brake was disconnected from the actuator and rested vertically. This Fishbed F was jacked up on the wing and fuselage to inspect the KT-92 (*Koleso Tarmaznoye*; Braked Wheel) main wheels. (Andrzej Morgala)

Polskie Wojsko Lotnicze (PWL; Polish Air Force) mechanics use a specially designed trolley to remove the MiG-21PFM's entire tail section for inspection. The open PT-21UK drag chute container is mounted immediately below the rudder. The open access panel just ahead of the national marking exposes the Orange SARPP flight recorder. This flight recorder was stowed upright on the MiG-21PFM, but was fitted horizontally on the later MiG-21MF. The fairing above the national marking accommodates the ID-2 induction sensor for the KSI-2 compass. MiG-21PFMs lacked the small button shaped antenna, which MiG-21MFs had mounted on the fairing rear. This fairing distinguished the MiG-21PFM tail from that of the MiG-21M/MF. (Andrzej Morgala)

The *Bulgarski Voyenno Vozdushni Sili* (BVVS; Bulgarian Air Force) carried out two modifications on their MiG-21PFM fleet during its service career. A Radome Green dielectric panel for the R-802V VHF multi-channel communications radio was installed on the tail tip. Additionally, a TS-27AMSh rear view mirror was mounted atop the canopy. This particular Fishbed F taxies past the apron of Ravnez Air Base, home of the 15. *Iztrebitelen Aviazionen Polk* (IAP: Fighter Aviation Regiment). (Stephan Boshniakov)

Fortele Aeriene ale Republicii Socialiste România (RARSR; Romanian Air Force) mechanics service the lower fuselage of a MiG-21PFM. The ventral fin's aft section was redesigned with the brake parachute container relocated from the left aft fuselage to the rudder base. Both the chute anchor and cable were removed from the MiG-21PFM's ventral fin. Nozzle cooling inlets for the R-11F2S-300 engine are placed on both left and right sides of the ventral fin. (Author's Collection)

The PWL's 2. *Pulk Lotnictwa Mysliwskiego 'Krakow'* (2nd Fighter Aviation Regiment 'Cracow') carried out its first operating from highways trials in 1972. Stretches of highways were closed to allow the MiG-21PFMs to take off and land from these roads. This tested the ability to disperse the fighters from air bases during wartime, when the bases were vulnerable to attack. Both MiG-21PFMs were retrofitted with Radome Green fin tip panels housing R-802V VHF multi-channel communications radios. Poland's Fishbed Fs were delivered without this dielectric panel and instead had an alloy fin tip panel. (Andrzej Morgala)

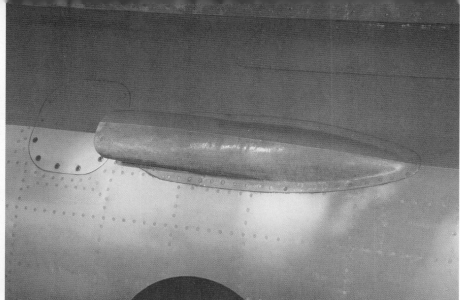

The MiG-21PFM's 5.3 м² (57.1-square-foot) vertical stabilizer had a wider chord than on the standard MiG-21PF. The PT-21UK brake parachute container was relocated from the lower left fuselage to the fin's base. The long afterburner cooling inlet is mounted above the Indian national marking on the aft fuselage.

A small avionics cooling inlet was only installed on the left tailfin. This duct was also mounted on the earlier MiG-21F-13 (Fishbed C) and MiG-21PF. Third-generation MiG-21s deleted the small inlet. The larger afterburner cooling inlet is located aft of and below the small duct.

Cooling air for the R-11F2S-300's afterburner was ducted through this long aft fuselage inlet. This inlet was also mounted on the right side. Both the MiG-21PF (Fishbed D) and MiG-21PFM (Fishbed F) employed this inlet.

A nozzle actuator cooling air inlet is located on both aft fuselage sides. The long, narrow fairing beside the duct covers the nozzle hydraulic lines. MiG-21s have stabilators (horizontal stabilizer/elevators), which moved on a single pivot point. Each stabilator has a +7°/-16.5° travel range.

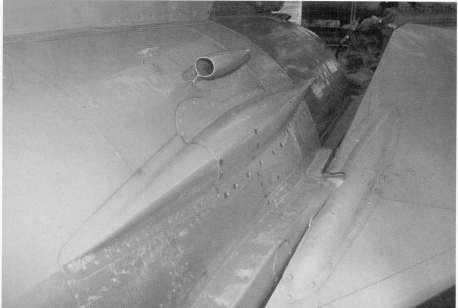

The PT-21UK brake parachute container houses a 19 м² (204.5 square-foot) brake parachute. The chute had a maximum release speed of 320 кмн (199 мрн) and was usually released when the MiG-21PFM was 1 м (3.3 feet) above the runway. The parachute fully deployed 1.5 seconds after it was released. The MiG-21PFM's PT-21UK was also mounted on late production MiG-21PFs.

The MiG-21PFM's Tumansky R-11F2S-300 engine employs a variable convergent nozzle. This nozzle is enclosed within a titanium aft fuselage shroud. The R-11F2S-300 turbojet engine had static thrust ratings of 8598 pounds dry and 13,613 pounds in afterburner. Stabilator fairings are mounted to both aft fuselage sides.

The SRO-2M *Khrom-Nikel* IFF system's three-pole antenna is mounted atop the MiG-21PFM's fin tip. A SOD-57M Air Traffic Control (ATC) transponder is located within the fin tip cone. This cone was painted Radome Green on operational Fishbed Fs, not the Silver on this aircraft at the *Technik Museum*. The position light and static discharger are located immediately below this cone.

A fuel dump pipe is mounted on the right side of the R-11F2S-300's inner nozzle. This pipe was not located on the left side. The MiG-21PFM pilot vented excess fuel through this pipe in an emergency, including lightening the aircraft for an emergency landing.

An LSK NVA (East German Air Force) MiG-21U-600 (Black 297/Serial Number 66 48 19) is prepared for a mission. The Mongol A lacked the instructor's aft canopy periscope mounted in later MiG-21 trainers. This variant also did not have the R-832 communications radio antenna mast on the aft dorsal spine. All MiG-21U trainers had enlarged dorsal spines compared to the fighter variants' smaller spines. A blind flying training curtain is fitted to the pupil's front cockpit. The small dielectric panel on the wing leading edge houses the SOD-57M ATC transponder. Beside this item are the landing light and the SRO-2M *Khrom-Nikel* IFF antenna. LSK NVA MiG-21Us had three digit Black numbers while fighters had Red numbers. (Hans-Joachim Mau)

A late production MiG-21U-600 (Red 2720/662720) of the PWL (Polish Air Force) prepares to taxi out to begin a mission. This Mongol A has the wide chord fin and a braking parachute housing on the base of the rudder, but lacks the aft canopy periscope housing. A ground crewman holds the crew access ladder he has just pulled from the aircraft. (Andrzej Morgala)

An LSK NVA MiG-21U-600 (Black 275/663219) assigned to *Flieger Ausbildungs Geschwader* (FAG; Pilot's Training Unit) 15 *'Heinz Kapelle'* at Rothenburg flies a mission. This Mongol A was assigned to the LSK NVA on 15 July 1966 and removed from service in March of 1990. The *Bundesluftwaffe* (West German Air Force) inventory number 23-92 was allocated to this particular trainer, but no Mongol ever entered *Bundesluftwaffe* service after German unification in 1990. (Hans-Joachim Mau)

This ex-Soviet MiG-21UM (Red 27) was impressed into the Georgian Air Force inventory. The Mongol B trainer retained its original VVS (Soviet Air Force) camouflage and tactical number. This MiG-21UM is parked at the airfield of Tbilaviamsheni Ltd, the former Soviet GAZ (State Aircraft Factory) 31 at Tbilisi. The former Georgian Soviet Socialist Republic, located in the Southern Caucasus region, became independent from the Soviet Union in 1990. (Marcus Fülber)

A *Letectvo Armady Ceske* (Czech Air Force after January of 1993) MiG-21US (Black 1048/10685148) taxis across the ramp. The instructor's periscope is deployed on the aft canopy. A Yellow aft fuselage band is painted on this natural metal Mongol B. The crest aft of the Black tactical number is for the 9. *Stihaci Letecky Pluk* (9th Fighter Aviation Regiment) at Bechyne Air Base. The Mongol B lacks the R-832 communications radio antenna mast on the rear dorsal spine. This antenna became standard on the subsequent MiG-21UM variant. The Czechs later scrapped Black 1048. (Sign via Roman Sekyrka)

US troops found this wrecked MiG-21UM (Blue 205/Serial Number 516963026) at Mogadishu airport, Somalia in December of 1992. It was one of eight Mongol Bs delivered to the *Dayuuradaha Xooga Dalka Somaliyeed* (DXDS; Somali Aeronautical Corps). The R-832 antenna mast was broken off the dorsal spine. American forces restoring order in war-torn Somalia sprayed AFEOD (for Air Force Explosive Ordnance Disposal) in Red on the nose. US troops later handed control in Somalia over to the United Nations. (Paul A. Jackson)

All MiG-21U trainers had the nose air data boom offset to the right, rather than center-mounted as on the MiG-21PF and MiG-21PFM fighters. Both this MiG-21U (Mongol A) and the later MiG-21US (Mongol B) had a TP-156M auxiliary air pressure tube mounted on the right nose side, immediately below the large avionics access panel. MiG-21UMs replaced this tube with a larger boom on the right nose. A small blister is incorporated into the access panel near the TP-156M tube. (Zdenek Hurt)

The instructor sat in the MiG-21US rear cockpit, which had identical instruments and controls to the front cockpit. Each cockpit had a separate canopy, which was hinged to the right. Cockpits on this MiG-21US are mostly Pale Peacock Blue. (Marcus Fülber)

A window separated the Mongol's front and rear cockpits. This protected the instructor in case the front canopy was lost. MiG-21Us had a larger single oval screen compared to the MiG-21US' window. The MiG-21US introduced KM-1 ejection seats in place of the Mongol A's SK seats. (Marcus Fülber)

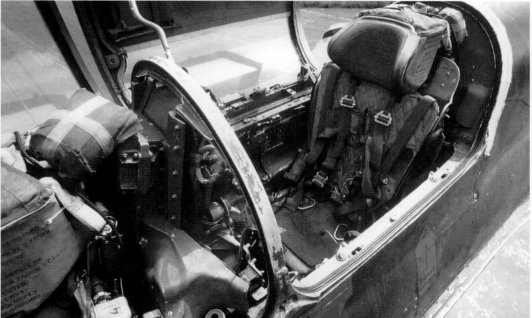

The front cockpit is opened on this LSK NVA MiG-21US (Black 250/Serial Number 01685148). The student pilot sat in this cockpit, with the instructor in the aft cockpit. All MiG-21U trainers lacked a radar scope in the cockpit. A Black SSh-45-100OS gun camera is mounted beside the ASP-PFD optical gun sight. This camera recorded firing runs for later study. (Marcus Fülber)

The throttle lever is mounted atop the left console of the MiG-21US' rear cockpit. Other controls and instruments are the same as in the front cockpit and on MiG-21 fighters. A Brown canvas sleeve holds oxygen hoses that are connected to the instructor's helmet before flight. (Marcus Fülber)

Radio and navigation controls are mounted on the right console and wall in the MiG-21US aft cockpit. A White hose near the instrument panel's right edge connected with a sealing hose mounted in the canopy when it was closed. Black radio and intercom cables are stowed along the cockpit wall. These are fitted to the pilot's helmet before flight. (Marcus Fülber)

The ventilator fan atop the instrument panel's right side was unique to the MiG-21 trainers' aft cockpit. This moved cooler air toward the instructor's body during hot conditions. MiG-21U instructors had highly restricted front views, which were helped by using the canopy-mounted periscope during taxiing, take offs, and landings. (Marcus Fülber)

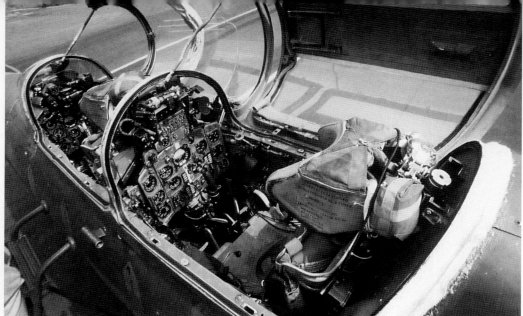

The MiG-21US had a periscope mounted in the upper centerline canopy. This provided the instructor with improved visibility during take off and landing. A venturi tube is mounted below the frame separating the front and rear cockpits. Heating tubes are imbedded into the front canopy glass to clear fogging from this surface. (Marcus Fülber)

The venturi tube was connected to the AD-6E cabin pressure regulation system. This tube was of a slightly different design from that installed on the MiG-21PFM fighter. The Red crew access ladder rests below the front cockpit sill. Orange and Black markings under the cockpit sills alerted ground crews to the canopy latches. (Marcus Fülber)

The MiG-21U was equipped with SK ejection seats and had a larger window between the pupil's and instructor's compartments. Later MiG-21UM and MiG-21US trainers had improved KM-1 ejection seats and smaller cockpit separation windows. The MiG-21U did not have the venturi tube mounted slightly below the left canopy on later Mongols. This variant was equipped with an ASP-5ND gun sight and a KAP-2K autopilot. An S-13-300-100 OS gun camera was mounted on the lower left wing surface, just beside the wing pylon. Both pilots wear the early GSh-6 helmet. A tarpaulin protects the left wing leading edge during crew access. (Andrzej Morgala)

A *Letectvo Ceskoslovenske Lidove Armady* (LCLA; Czechoslovak People's Army Air Force) MiG-21U (Black 4916/664916) sits on the ramp. Both this variant and the later MiG-21US lacked the DVA-3A Angle of Attack (AoA) sensor, which was mounted on the MiG-21UM's left nose. The large fuselage fuel tank is located within the fairing immediately aft of the canopy. The MiG-21U had an internal fuel capacity of 2350 L (621gallons). (Zdenek Titz)

Several MiG-21Us – including this Hungarian Mongol A – were fitted with an S-13-300-100 OS gun camera. This was mounted on the lower left wing, outboard of the wing pylon. MiG-21U trainers lacked any internal armament, but they had provision for one pod-mounted 12.7ᴍᴍ A-12.7 machine gun with ammunition on the centerline pylon.

This *Polskie Wojsko Lotnicze* (PWL; Polish Air Force) MiG-21UM (Red 7503/03695175) is serviced between missions. Red protective covers are fitted over the engine inlet and the DVA-3A AoA sensor on the left nose. The DVA-3A provided input to the AP-155 three-axis autopilot. The lower nose location of the SRD-5 (NATO designation High Fix) radar rangefinder's temperature probe is unique to the MiG-21U trainers. A Radome Green fiberglass disc covering the ARK-10 Automatic Direction Finder (ADF) antenna is located just ahead of the nose wheel well. All Mongol variants have KT-102 nose wheels and KT-92 main wheels. (Andrzej Morgala)

Aero built this MiG-21F-13 (Black 0418) at Vodochody, near Prague, for the *Letectvo Ceskoslovenske Lidove Armady* (LCLA: Czechoslovak People's Army Air Force). Czechoslovak-built Fishbed Cs replaced the clear aft canopy section with metal skinning. Aero completed 194 MiG-21F-13s for the LCLA between February of 1962 and June of 1972.

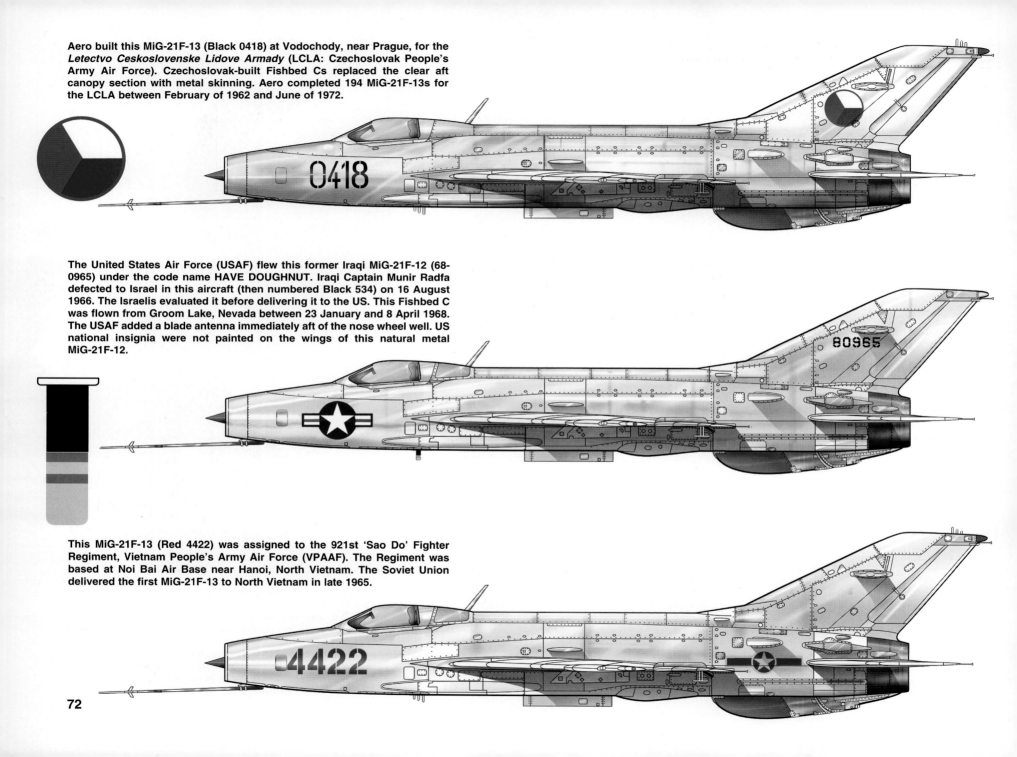

The United States Air Force (USAF) flew this former Iraqi MiG-21F-12 (68-0965) under the code name HAVE DOUGHNUT. Iraqi Captain Munir Radfa defected to Israel in this aircraft (then numbered Black 534) on 16 August 1966. The Israelis evaluated it before delivering it to the US. This Fishbed C was flown from Groom Lake, Nevada between 23 January and 8 April 1968. The USAF added a blade antenna immediately aft of the nose wheel well. US national insignia were not painted on the wings of this natural metal MiG-21F-12.

This MiG-21F-13 (Red 4422) was assigned to the 921st 'Sao Do' Fighter Regiment, Vietnam People's Army Air Force (VPAAF). The Regiment was based at Noi Bai Air Base near Hanoi, North Vietnam. The Soviet Union delivered the first MiG-21F-13 to North Vietnam in late 1965.

The *Bulgarski Voyenno Vozdushni Sili* (BVVS; Bulgarian Air Force) camouflaged this MiG-21PF (White 20) for ground attack operations. The Fishbed D's upper surfaces were in a uniquely Bulgarian scheme of Dark Green, Light Green, and Tan, while the undersurfaces were Pale Blue. Bulgarian national insignia appeared on the vertical tail, aft fuselage, and wing upper and lower surfaces.

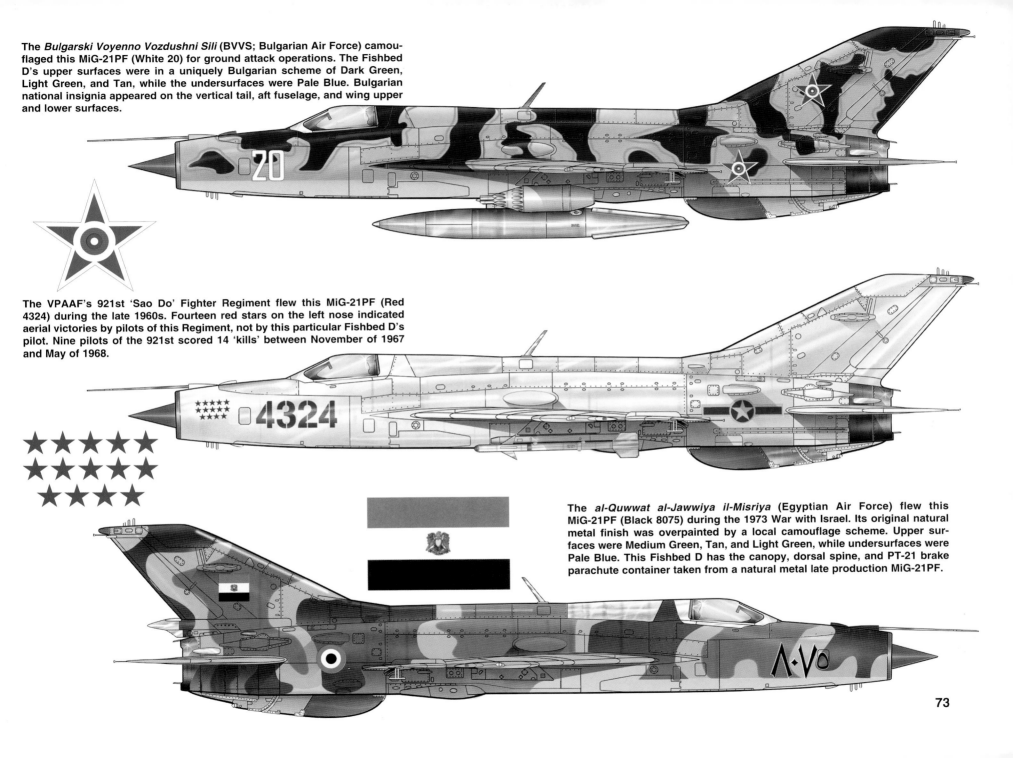

The VPAAF's 921st 'Sao Do' Fighter Regiment flew this MiG-21PF (Red 4324) during the late 1960s. Fourteen red stars on the left nose indicated aerial victories by pilots of this Regiment, not by this particular Fishbed D's pilot. Nine pilots of the 921st scored 14 'kills' between November of 1967 and May of 1968.

The *al-Quwwat al-Jawwiya il-Misriya* (Egyptian Air Force) flew this MiG-21PF (Black 8075) during the 1973 War with Israel. Its original natural metal finish was overpainted by a local camouflage scheme. Upper surfaces were Medium Green, Tan, and Light Green, while undersurfaces were Pale Blue. This Fishbed D has the canopy, dorsal spine, and PT-21 brake parachute container taken from a natural metal late production MiG-21PF.

This MiG-21F-12 (MG-34/740404) was assigned to *Hävittäjälentolaivue* (HävLLv; Fighter Squadron) 31, *Ilmavoimat* (Finnish Air Force) at Rissala, Finland. It was a downgraded export variant of the MiG-21F-13 flown by the Soviet and Warsaw Pact air forces. The MiG-21F-12 lacked the SRO-2 *Khrom* (NATO designation Odd Rods) IFF system's three-pole antenna and the Radome Green SOD-57M ATC transponder bar on the vertical tail. Additionally, this variant was not equipped with the *Sirena* 2 radar warning receiver and its associated fin tip fairing. The last Finnish MiG-21F-12 was retired on 17 January 1986. (Klaus Niska)

The United States Air Force (USAF) and US Navy evaluated the former Iraqi Air Force MiG-21F-12 (68-0965; ex-Black 534) at Groom Lake, Nevada. The first tests were conducted under the code name HAVE DOUGHNUT between 23 January and 8 April 1968. The Black number 80965 was painted on the vertical stabilizer. A US-made VHF/Tactical Air Navigation (Tacan) blade antenna was mounted under the nose. The Israeli government loaned this Fishbed C to the US for testing in late 1967. (Robert F. Dorr)

A Polish ground crew works on a 'contaminated' MiG-21F-13 during an exercise. These soldiers all wore L-2 chemical protection suits. No national markings were painted on the upper wing surfaces, which was typical for Warsaw Pact air forces until the mid-1970s. Poland's initial MiG-21F-13s were assigned to the 1. *Pulk Lotnictwa Mysliwskiego 'Warszawa'* (1st Fighter Aviation Regiment 'Warsaw') and were first publicly displayed on 12 September 1963. (Andrzej Morgala)

The USAF-operated MiG-21F-12 (68-0965) only with US national markings on the nose, not on the upper and lower wing surfaces. Iraqi pilot Captain Munir Radfa defected in this Fishbed C to Tel Nof Air Base, Israel on 16 August 1966. This MiG-21F-12 lacked the three-pole SRO-2 *Khrom* IFF system antenna and the fin tip blister for the *Sirena* 2 radar warning receiver. Captain Radfa later emigrated to a Western country and died in 1998. This MiG-21F-12 was returned to Israel and is now displayed at the Israel Defense Force/Air Force Museum at Hatzerim. (Robert F. Dorr)

This MiG-21PF (White 121) was assigned to a *Voenno Vozdushnye Sili* (VVS; Soviet Air Force) training unit. Aircraft in such units received three-digit tactical numbers. This MiG-21PF has its number in a broken White outline on the camouflage finish. This Fishbed D is believed to have Dark Green, Green, and Tan upper surfaces and Pale Blue undersurfaces. It was retrofitted with a gun gas deflector plate below the fuselage auxiliary inlet door. (Sergej F. Sergejev)

A late production VVS MiG-21PF Fishbed F (Blue 66) taxis out for a mission. This sub-variant has the PT-21UK brake parachute container at the rudder base and a wider chord vertical stabilizer. Standard production MiG-21PFs had narrow chord vertical stabilizers and did not have the PT-21UK containers. (G.F. Petrov)

A FARSR (Romanian Air Force) MiG-21PF (Red 501/761501) awaits permission for take off, while a MiG-21M (Fishbed J) is about to land. The MiG-21PF is armed with a UB-16-57U pod containing sixteen 57MM unguided S-5 rockets on the left wing pod. An identical pod is likely mounted on the right wing pylon. (Author's Collection)

The *Flugzeugwerke* (Aircraft Factory) at Dresden, Germany overhauled this and five other ex-East German MiG-21PFs in 1989. They were intended for export to the Iranian *Pasdaran* (Islamic Revolutionary Guards Corps) Air Force; however, the German Democratic Republic's dissolution on 3 October 1990 prevented delivery to Iran. These MiG-21PFs were camouflaged with Olive Drab and Sand-Yellow upper surfaces at the factory, but no Iranian national markings were applied before delivery. (Wolfgang Tamme)

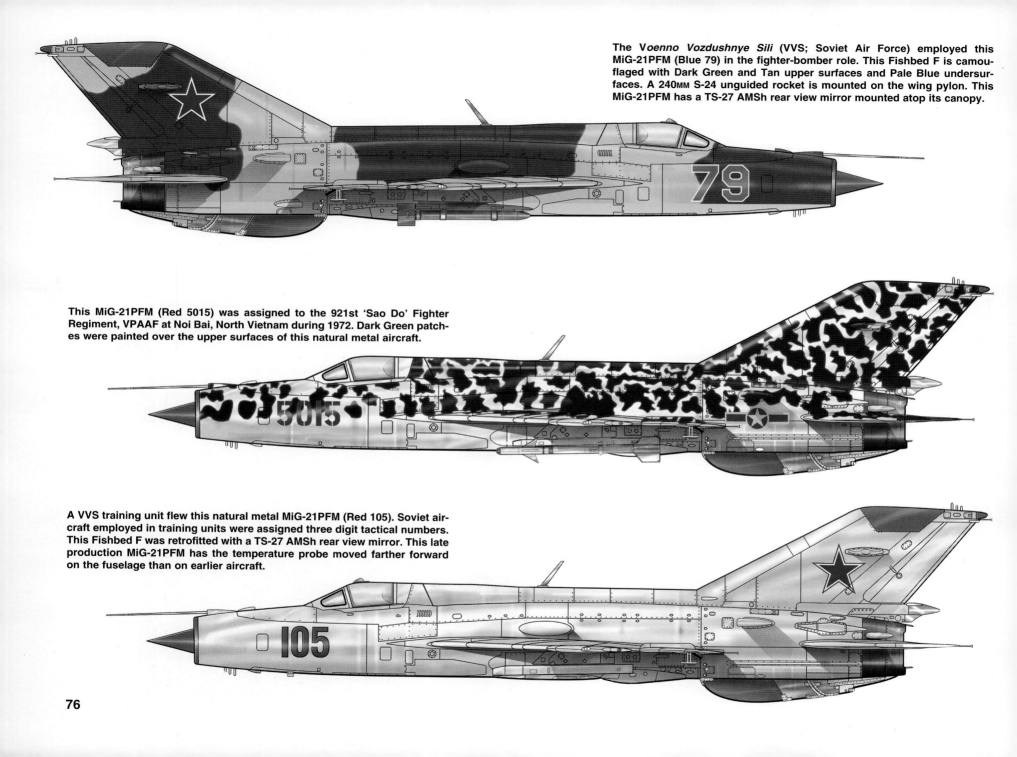

The *Voenno Vozdushnye Sili* (VVS; Soviet Air Force) employed this MiG-21PFM (Blue 79) in the fighter-bomber role. This Fishbed F is camouflaged with Dark Green and Tan upper surfaces and Pale Blue undersurfaces. A 240MM S-24 unguided rocket is mounted on the wing pylon. This MiG-21PFM has a TS-27 AMSh rear view mirror mounted atop its canopy.

This MiG-21PFM (Red 5015) was assigned to the 921st 'Sao Do' Fighter Regiment, VPAAF at Noi Bai, North Vietnam during 1972. Dark Green patches were painted over the upper surfaces of this natural metal aircraft.

A VVS training unit flew this natural metal MiG-21PFM (Red 105). Soviet aircraft employed in training units were assigned three digit tactical numbers. This Fishbed F was retrofitted with a TS-27 AMSh rear view mirror. This late production MiG-21PFM has the temperature probe moved farther forward on the fuselage than on earlier aircraft.

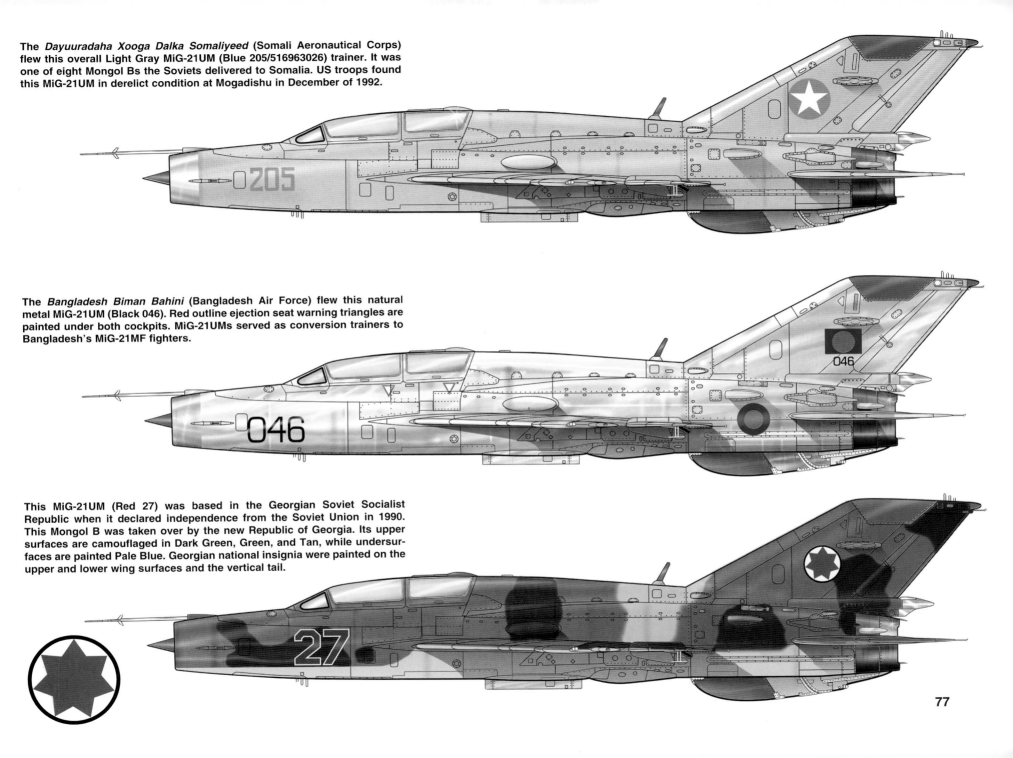

The *Dayuuradaha Xooga Dalka Somaliyeed* (Somali Aeronautical Corps) flew this overall Light Gray MiG-21UM (Blue 205/516963026) trainer. It was one of eight Mongol Bs the Soviets delivered to Somalia. US troops found this MiG-21UM in derelict condition at Mogadishu in December of 1992.

The *Bangladesh Biman Bahini* (Bangladesh Air Force) flew this natural metal MiG-21UM (Black 046). Red outline ejection seat warning triangles are painted under both cockpits. MiG-21UMs served as conversion trainers to Bangladesh's MiG-21MF fighters.

This MiG-21UM (Red 27) was based in the Georgian Soviet Socialist Republic when it declared independence from the Soviet Union in 1990. This Mongol B was taken over by the new Republic of Georgia. Its upper surfaces are camouflaged in Dark Green, Green, and Tan, while undersurfaces are painted Pale Blue. Georgian national insignia were painted on the upper and lower wing surfaces and the vertical tail.

A camouflaged *Voenno Vozdushnye Sili* (VVS; Soviet Air Force) MiG-21PFM (Blue 79) is refuelled prior to its next mission. This Fishbed F was equipped with a TS-27AMSh rear view mirror in the canopy roof. The fighter was delivered in natural metal, but the Soviets later camouflaged it with Green and Tan on the upper surfaces and Pale Blue on the undersurfaces. (G.F. Petrov)

Another VVS MiG-21PFM Fishbed F (Blue 79) sits on its hardstand. The national markings on the tail fin appear highly worn, while those on the nearby Fishbed F are in a much better condition. This MiG-21PFM carries the 490 L (129-gallon) centerline fuel tank, which could be safely flown at speeds up to Mach 1. (G.F. Petrov)

This VVS MiG-21PFM (Red 31) is parked on a ramp at a Soviet air base. It is a late production Fishbed F, which had the TS-27AMSh rear view mirror and Radome Green vertical stabilizer dielectric panel for the R-802V VHF multi-channel communications radio. Angled blast deflectors behind the ramp are standard at Russian (formerly Soviet) airfields. Soviet tactical aircraft normally operated from ramps during peacetime operations. (G.F. Petrov)

A MiG-21PFM (Red 105) lifts off from a runway. Three-digit tactical numbers are typical for VVS training units, while operational units assigned two-digit numbers to their aircraft. This late production MiG-21PFM has the TS-27AMSh rear view mirror and the Radome Green R-802V radio panel on the upper vertical stabilizer. (G.F. Petrov)

This MiG-21US (Red 578) was assigned to the 393rd Training Fighter Aviation Regiment, Afghan Army Air Force at Mazar-e-Sharif. The vertical stabilizer displays the national insignia introduced in 1982: a Red star on a White disc with (from center) Green, Red, and Black rings. A tarpaulin secured over the canopy protected it against the sun. The MiG-21US's right pylon has an APU-13 missile rail for the R-3S (AA-2 Atoll) infrared homing air-to-air missile. (Wojciech Luczak)

This MiG-21UM (White 24) is assigned to the 19. *Iztrebitelen Aviazionen Polk* (IAP; Fighter Aviation Regiment), *Bulgarski Voyenno Vozdushni Sili* (BVVS; Bulgarian Air Force). The Regiment is based at Graf Ignatievo near Plovdiv in Western Bulgaria. It has a unique camouflage of Sand Brown and Olive Drab upper surfaces, with Pale Blue undersurfaces. Post-Communist Bulgarian national markings painted on the vertical stabilizer were adopted in 1992. These consisted of a White center disc, Red inner ring, Green outer ring, and a thin White outline (Stephan Boshniakov)

A VVS MiG-21UM (Blue 86) is parked at Kupiansk Air Base near Kharkov in the Ukrainian Soviet Socialist Republic (now Ukraine). The thin White outline to the tactical number was a common practice within VVS Regiments. The Red crew access ladder propped against the forward fuselage is standard for all MiG-21 variants. (Sergej F. Sergejev)

The *Bangladesh Biman Bahini* (Bangladesh Air Force) operated this MiG-21UM (Black 046). Its tactical number was repeated in Black below the fin flash, which was common among Bangladesh's MiG-21UMs and MiG-21MFs. An antenna mast for the R-832 communications radio is mounted on the Mongol B's rear dorsal spine. MiG-21 fighter variants did not have this antenna mast. (Peter Steinemann)

Fight's On!
More Combat Jets from squadron/signal publications

5501 F-16 Fighting Falcon

5503 F-14 Tomcat

5506 B-52 Stratofortress

5518 F/A-18 Hornet

5521 F-86 Sabre

5528 F-15 Eagle

1065 F-4 Phantom II

1070 F-8 Crusader

1185 F-105 Thunderchief

For more information on squadron/signal publications, go to www.squadron.com